Elementary
Teacher's
Art Ideas
Desk Book

GRETCHEN S. SANDERSON

PARKER PUBLISHING COMPANY, INC.
WEST NYACK, NEW YORK

©1974 by

PARKER PUBLISHING COMPANY, INC.

West Nyack, New York

Library of Congress Cataloging in Publication Data

Sanderson, Gretchen S
   Elementary teacher's art ideas desk book.

   1. Art—Study and teaching (Elementary)
2. Creative activities and seat work. I. Title.
N350.S27   372.5'044   73-19864
ISBN 0-13-260679-8

To my husband, Bill, and my family,
Wilma, Eunice, Sheila, and Byron

A Word from the Author

During my career as an art teacher in both public and private schools, I have had enjoyable associations with numerous elementary teachers. Daily experiences with these teachers, who repeatedly requested new art ideas, different approaches, and special projects, motivated me to compile a resource desk book for them. As travelling art supervisor and in-school art consultant, it was my experience that teachers' needs grow to extensive proportions. This desk book is designed to serve these needs, providing hundreds of fully illustrated, step-by-step lessons in many different media.

For instance, puppet making, always a favorite in the elementary grades, is presented in chapter 1. Here you will find several methods of constructing puppets, from the simple, folded-paper puppets appropriate for kindergarteners to the more complex, life-size paper puppets for older children. Each lesson here, as well as throughout the book, calls for easily obtainable and inexpensive materials within the reach of any art budget.

Since masks are often in demand, studies in design in cultural groups and masks for plays and individual seasonal fun are clearly covered in chapter 5.

I found teachers eager to display their children's art work in different and original ways for P.T.A. or bulletin board displays. Chapter 9 describes both simple and more complex methods to show off the children's work in the classroom and for the proud parents.

Clear steps in the process of printmaking are illustrated in chapter 14, "Proud Prints." The simplest thumb print to more advanced techniques, such as collagraphs and three-color monoprints, are carefully explained in this section. All of these methods have stood the test of classroom use with great success.

Making gifts can be an interesting and functional activity as a result of an art lesson in a variety of media. Such gifts can be found in chapter 17 where popular materials such as plaster of Paris, pariscraft, and even window screening make unusual and delightful gifts. The study of mobiles, stabiles, and kinetics in chapter 20 covers directions in simple construction for exploring the principles of kinetics on the grade school level. These and many more types of lessons are offered in this handy desk book.

Art lessons can become valuable when the potential of the medium is understood, and this is why the teacher needs to know how to organize the class, prepare the work area, clarify the objective involved in the lesson, and anticipate the clean-up time. A well-organized lesson can be a successful one, and material often dreaded, such as plaster of Paris, can become an enjoyable experience for everyone. The introduction of a new medium in easy-to-understand language need not be frightening nor postponed when a little experimentation can give the pupils a new activity—a change from drawing and painting. Pariscraft, for example, can be handled carelessly or to advantage depending on preparation, organization, actual manipulation, and cleanup.

A special section in the beginning of this book, Helpful Hints and Shortcuts, should be read by the teacher before attempting any of the lessons. These suggestions have been developed through trial and error, resulting in a collection of easy steps to take for the successful use of classroom materials and methods.

At the end of each chapter in the book you will find a section of ten briefly explained bonus ideas. The introduction to these extra activities is just enough to stimulate your imagination so you can develop a simplified or advanced version of the lesson especially geared for your particular class.

The teacher who feels inadequate in the area of art will soon be set at ease by the variety of clearly explained lessons in this book. To promote confidence by offering a multitude of materials, methods, and results is one of the major purposes of this book. As an added benefit, teachers themselves will gain an increased sense of art appreciation through the ideas presented in this book, fostering individual growth in art courses, such as graphics and sculpture.

Elementary Teacher's Art Ideas Desk Book can also be used outside of the classroom in the scouts, summer camps, special education classes, and even at home for parents interested in creating activities for their children.

I trust my enthusiasm in preparing this book will be contagious to all who open its covers to enter the world of art expression.

Gretchen S. Sanderson

Helpful Hints and Shortcuts

After years of teaching experience on all levels, I have learned, through trial and error, helpful hints and shortcuts that I hope will be of value to classroom teachers. If teachers could set aside a few minutes to consider the characteristics of materials, ways to prolong the life of tools, and basic items to have within reach, lessons could be relieved of many problems that arise without these reminders.

It is with the objectives of good preparation and organization of lessons that the following pointers are presented.

"Vaseline" Petroleum Jelly

"Vaseline" Petroleum Jelly has many uses and is a vital material to keep on hand in the classroom. First, it is an excellent first-aid treatment for finger cuts. Second, any container with a screw-on top that contains glue, varnish, or shellac should, upon first opening it, have "Vaseline" Petroleum Jelly applied to both inside cover and rim. This prevents the top from adhering and making the container impossible to open.

Waxed Paper

No classroom should be without waxed paper; it has both practical and artistic uses. It can be used as an art lesson simply by placing it over a line drawing on white paper. With a pencil trace the drawing underneath on the waxed paper, transferring the wax line to the paper. Watercolor washes can be painted over the drawing leaving white lines where the wax resists the color.

Waxed paper is also ideal to use where the material you are working with is apt to stick to newspaper. Place sheets of waxed paper over the desk or on top of newspaper and pour plaster of Paris freeform designs. The plaster will not stick to this surface. Waxed paper also makes beautiful window parchments or flowers. It is a must for classroom art activities.

7

Plastic Bags, Large and Small

Both waxed paper and plastic bags now on the market are in demand for art lessons because of their practical and decorative uses. When sticky objects or freshly painted pieces must be transferred to another drying place, a small plastic bag covering the hand makes the move neat and clean. Larger bags are handy for spraying papier-mâché with quick-drying enamel. They cover the arm to the elbow and prevent any spray from getting on the skin or damaging clothing. Much less expensive than ready-made plastic gloves, they serve the same purpose admirably.

As with waxed paper, plastic bags have a great deal of potential as art projects in themselves. Slightly filled with air they work well as unusual mobiles. They also lend themselves to creative flower-making and transparencies.

Newspapers

All elementary teachers know the value of keeping plenty of newspaper on hand. In addition to covering work areas, newspapers can be made into temporary aprons for painting lessons. Also, crayon work yields far brighter results with a thin pad of newspaper underneath.

To keep the supply of newspaper at a high level, have each child bring in a newspaper for his art lesson. Not only will this teach the children responsibility, but it will relieve the teacher of an extra task.

Plastic Spoons

Plastic spoons are inexpensive so each child can bring one for himself or help contribute to the classroom supply. They are a good size to use with plaster of Paris and when plaster has dried on the spoon it can be easily pushed off ready and clean for another lesson. The use of plastic spoons also encourages the children, with direction, to lift out paint with a spoon and not a paintbrush, which often happens if there isn't a tool handy to remove poster paint.

Dish-Water Detergent

Detergent is often thought of only as a household product, but it is a must in the classroom, especially for older groups using oil-base paints. It has also been used successfully when working with plasticine. Both oil-base ink and oil paints are hard to remove from the skin, but with a little dish-water detergent poured into the palm of the hand and rubbed into the skin it comes off with surprising ease. To prevent plasticine from clinging under the fingernails, before the art lesson simply work the detergent around the cuticles and under the nails. Let it dry, work with plasticine, and when through, simply wash the hands well in the detergent, and they will feel free of stickiness.

Clothesline

If you do not have space for a permanent clothesline, then an area suitable for hanging up drawings to dry should be arranged for. Place the hooks so a rope can quickly be attached where heads won't bump the drawings and drafts won't blow them around. Prints especially need a drying place; the line can also double as exhibition space if bulletin boards are limited.

Plasticine

This nonhardening clay has different trade names and is frequently used on the grade-school level. Try using the dish-water detergent before and after an art activity with this medium, as explained in the paragraph on detergents. Experiment with and without this coating before you have a plasticine lesson. Always experiment with any material or lesson before presenting it to the class.

Paper Sculpture

Curling paper is a common method used in paper sculpture. The best way to prevent tearing the paper is to curl it over a pencil rather than curling it with a scissor blade. So many times children will try scissor curling when pencils in various sizes could create a wider variety of forms.

Paper Folding and Cutting

Paper folding involves basic fundamentals and, when followed carefully, accurate and neat paper work results. First, the paper should be placed flat on the desk. The edge nearest the pupil is lifted up to the top edge with corners matched. Place one hand flat on the middle to hold the paper in place and put the other hand next to it. Keeping the hands flat on the paper, move them away from the center. (See Figure A) This results in a neatly folded piece of paper. Make a cartoon of paper folded the right way to remind the children how much easier it is than doing it the wrong way, that is, folding the paper in the air on the fold. (Figure B)

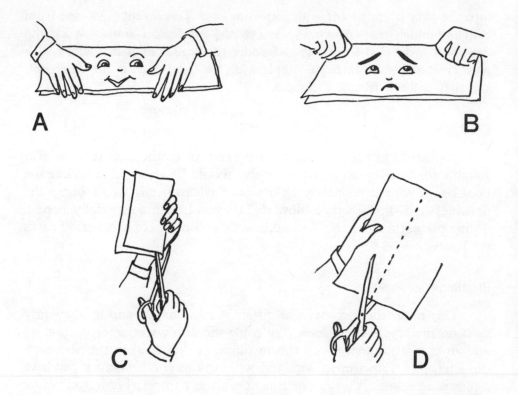

Cutting paper also has basic fundamentals. After the paper has been folded, do not hold it in the air and cut while folded. (Figure C) This only results in a ragged edge and a struggle to guide the scissors to prevent cutting the fingers. The best way is to open the paper and then cut on the crease. (Figure D)

Pariscraft

Pariscraft is now so popular that you will undoubtedly want to use it in the classroom. However, it is a medium that should be handled with care. Tearing is not advised, since it creates a dust that can be injurious to a child's lungs, especially if the pupil is allergic to dust or has asthma. In addition, the plaster is being wasted since the particles of plaster are the basis of pariscraft; they should not be discarded. Often pariscraft has to be cut while damp; keep scissors clean and dry after such use to prevent the blades from rusting. This type of lesson has to be especially well preplanned and organized to make it enjoyable and wasteless. Always prepare a short, easy-to-do lesson with a minimum of pariscraft as an introduction to this medium.

In preparing pariscraft for use remember the following vital points. Cut the pariscraft strips ahead of time when you have a rough estimation of the amount needed. It is better to have extra strips left over than to have to stop frequently to cut more. Set these dry strips where they have no chance of getting wet. This is extremely important because when water has dried on pariscraft it will not reactivate, in other words, it becomes hard and will not soften for use. Use warm water for dipping the pariscraft strips. Teach the pupils to gently squeeze the water out of the material to prevent the plaster from being thrown away in the excess water. Some plaster will collect in the bottom of the bowl; this can be used on the finished piece to achieve a smoother finish. Do not pour water with plaster particles down the classroom sink. Let it settle overnight in a can, pour off the excess water the next day, and discard the can with the residue. Since pariscraft tends to dry out the skin, use a few drops of hand lotion after the lesson or use the detergent procedure described earlier. Needless to say, aprons are essential for craft lessons in this medium.

Straw Blowing

The unpredictable results achieved through straw blowing can provide an interesting art lesson, but without preplanning it can turn into a great disappointment. For best results make sure the poster paint is not too heavy to begin with. Most of the time the teacher should prepare the paint in advance, however, with a smaller or older group of pupils the children themselves can be taught how to do this. Ideally the paint should flow easily and be free of lumps. The paper used is also very important. Select a paper with a smooth surface so the paint will not be retarded in its progress. Another helpful hint is to hold the straw, preferably the jumbo size, at an angle to the paper, not directly on top of the paint. The idea is to let the stream of air flow down the straw to the edge of the puddle of paint so it will gently move out in different directions. If the straw is held incorrectly the child will have to blow too hard, which is not the way it is to be done. This is a fun lesson in observation of color mixture that teaches how the three primary colors blend to form secondary colors.

Collage Boxes

Every elementary teacher should keep a large box in the classroom for left-over materials that can be used for collage work. The ecological principle of recycling can be applied right in the classroom by keeping such a collage box.

Brushes

Children are never too young to learn how to care for their art materials and tools. This is especially true in a classroom where supplies must be shared and stretched for maximum use. When it comes to the care and maintenance of paintbrushes the nondirective approach does not apply; no matter how much freedom the child is given, mistreated brushes will not help him create better pictures. A brush needs care both in actual use and in cleanup. The pupils should be instructed in the proper application of the brush to paper to avoid "scrubbing," which quickly wears out the bristles. For clean-up, tin cans should be set up at the sinks and the children taught to thoroughly rinse their brushes, standing them upright with the bristles in the air to dry. Discourage the children from twisting and wringing the bristles in paper toweling. A cartoon drawing can be easily made for display at the sink to teach proper brush care in an enjoyable way. Figure E shows a sad, misused brush with its bristles spread apart, while the cartoon in Figure F illustrates a happy brush with bristles straight and clean.

E   F

Supplies in General

To develop more confidence in the use of materials and art implements the elementary teacher will find it worthwhile to experiment with the materials involved in each lesson before presenting it to the class. Actually go through the steps of the lesson to determine the amount of time needed for completion, the supplies and amounts of each type, the size of the work area, where you can display the finished pieces, and the objectives of the lesson.

Contents

CHAPTER 1

Playful Puppets

*A*ll children love play acting, either as individuals or in a group. Puppet characters of all sizes and shapes can easily be made from a variety of materials, from the simplest folded paper type to complicated marionettes.

The educational value of puppet making is far-reaching for it includes designing, construction, sewing, manipulation, and integration with school curriculum.

Anticipation, participation, and observation are equally enjoyable in the art of puppetry.

Lesson 1   Floppy the Puppet

Objectives

Floppy the Puppet is a quiet, small desk puppet ideal for kindergarten and first grade. The materials are few, the construction easy, and the manipulation fun. Floppy can be used to act out stories, dance to music, and be ready to obey any command.

Materials

Strips and scraps of white paper, string, scissors, paste, crayons.

Procedure

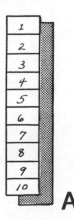

A

- Hold two strips of paper together and fold into 10 sections. (Figure A)
- Open and place back to back and glue sections 5 and 6 together.

17

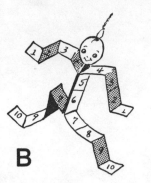

B

C

- Bend some of the fold to take the position of arms and legs. (Figure B)
- Place two squares of paper together; bending back the corners, cut an oval for the head and glue on these flaps. (Figure C)
- Insert the neck in the body and glue in place.
- Add a string to the top of the head and Floppy is ready to bounce away either on the desk or floor.
- Make this puppet in all sizes for different characters to act out a play or line up for a musical.

Lesson 2   Life-size Paper Puppet

Objectives

A life-size paper puppet offers many facets of learning. It can develop an awareness of body proportions, provide a study in color and design, and teach good-grooming lessons. These puppets have even added to a successful P.T.A. evening, where parents found paper duplicates of their children sitting quietly in their children's seats. This automatically omits the question, "Where does Jimmy sit?" A mirror is an essential part of the lesson, affording the children freedom to study their coloring, features, and dress. A child's self-portrait often has a striking resemblance to the contour of his head, eyeglasses, a lost tooth, and even freckles. This project can span three lessons, culminating in the assembly of the entire puppet, ready for the P.T.A., a classroom parade, or an exhibition.

Materials

Three sheets of white 9″ x 12″ paper, 1 sheet of 12″ x 18″ white paper, mirror, 4 strips of crepe paper each 18″ long (either flesh-colored, black, or brown), stapler, crayons.

Procedure

- Hold a sheet of 9″ x 12″ white paper vertically in front of you. Starting with the head, discuss features and proportions. Ask the children one at a time to go to the mirror and study his or her face. (Figure A)
- Mark off for the chin about one-quarter inch from the bottom of the paper.
- Draw an oval for the head just inside the edges, so ears and hair can be added. Add the neck. Complete the coloring. (Figure B) Then cut it out.
- Begin the hands. Hold the 9″ x 12″ paper in front of you horizontally, and placing the left hand on the paper with fingers slightly open, draw around it with the right hand. Repeat with the right hand. (Figure C) Color and cut out.
- For the shoes, place the paper horizontally on the floor and step on it with the left foot. Draw around it. Repeat with the right foot. (Figure D) Color and cut out.

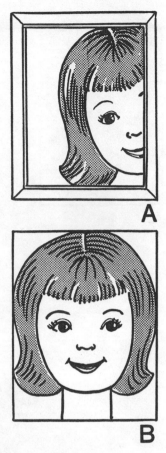

A

B

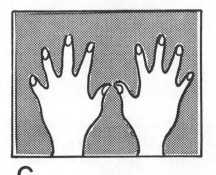

C

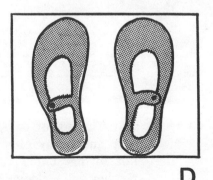

D

- Now start the body. Holding the 12″ x 18″ white paper vertically in front of you, fold the bottom part up to touch the top edge, folding it in half. The half

E

fold represents the waist, so cut a short triangle at each edge. Since our shoulders are not square, cut off the top corners. The body is ready if it is to be a girl. (Figure E) If it is a boy cut a triangle out to look like shorts. The children can look in the mirror again to copy their clothes.

- Count the number of buttons and add a name tag.
- Staple the neck to the body, the hands to crepe-paper arms and the shoes to the crepe-paper legs. (Figure F)
- The twin puppet is now ready to sit at a child's desk, and with his hands taped to the desk and his neck supported he is waiting for the parents to arrive for a P.T.A. classroom visit. (Figure G)

F

G

Lesson 3   Lunch Bag Puppet

Objectives

The square-base, stand-up brown lunch bag makes an easy and funny puppet to be manipulated by hand. It does not involve either cutting or pasting, hence the classroom teacher will welcome this no-paste lesson. This puppet can be used as a hand or stand-alone puppet merely by stuffing it slightly with crumpled paper. Several of these would be handy to provide fun and entertainment for little actors on rainy days.

Materials

Brown square-base bags, crayons.

Procedure

- Place the bag closed with its flap side on top and the open end of the bag nearest you on the desk.
- Draw a round face, including ears, so it touches the two sides and top and continue the face below the flap. Draw a smiling mouth below the flap, and add eyes, hair, nose, and eyebrows above it.
- Round the shoulders to the edge of the bag, color in his or her suit and add a name tag. Color the mouth bright red. (Figure A)
- Open the flap and continue the face to the top edge. (Figure B)

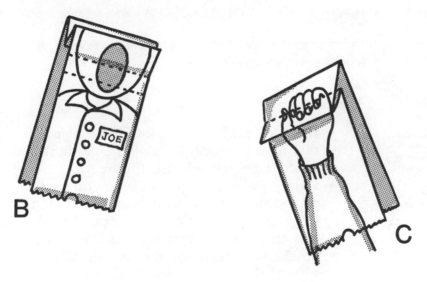

- Continue the mouth in bright red in a large oval shape.
- To manipulate the talking puppet, slide your hand gently into bag without opening it too much. Curl your fingers down into the flap and move it up and down. (Figure C) The puppet begins to talk!

Lesson 4   Pariscraft Animal Hand Puppet

Objectives

Pariscraft is an effective medium in this two-part imaginary animal hand puppet. It offers the pupil an introduction to pariscraft that "Pop" artists use in their sculpture of people and objects. Since this puppet is entirely imaginative, a great deal of freedom is involved. Another advantage is the small amount of material required. This two-part animal hand puppet can be used as separate parts, or a strip of pariscraft can be used to hold them together in the palm of the hand. It also is excellent for sound, for when clapped together a clear, loud click is heard.

Materials

Pariscraft, bowl of water, scissors, newspapers, paints (either poster or acrylic).

Procedure

- If the left hand is to be used for the puppet, then use that hand to model on. Hold it in a slightly curved, closed-finger, relaxed pose. (Figure A)
- Lightly wrap cut strips of pariscraft dipped in water around the hand up to the knuckles. Flare the ends up to give the effect of mane or ears (this also makes it easier to slip on the hand). Use at least three layers.
- Do the same with the thumb, but leave it a little wider at the knuckle. This will dry in twelve minutes. Add eyes and other features. (Figure B)
- Clap together either with music or just let them "talk."

A

B

Lesson 5   Sectional Alligator Puppet

Objectives

Learning the art of the puppeteer takes time and practice; however, a little understanding of maneuvering can be experienced with sectional animal puppets. The cardboard tube discarded from paper towels makes a good base. Cutting one into sections and joining the pieces with colored tissue allows a simulation of the swaying movements of the alligator. A long green head, protruding eyes, and a red mouth can look very realistic. Attaching strings to head and hips and pulling in opposite directions really makes the alligator move. Large sheets of brown wrapping paper can be painted with scenes of water and shoreline, and the study of the alligator's habitat can make a complete and interesting lesson.

Materials

Cardboard tube, green-colored tissue paper, waterproof glue, scissors, red and green construction paper, string.

Procedure

- Cut the tube into 4 sections and join them together with green tissue paper leaving them 1" apart.
- Cut tail, head, and feet from green construction paper and glue them in place. Line the mouth with red paper.
- Add eyes and strings. (Figure A)

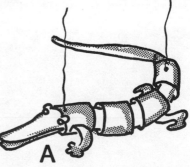

- To make the puppet heavier, press lumps of plasticine in the first and last sections—this will make him drag along the ground.
- Now make him crawl along by manipulating the strings.

Lesson 6   Balloon and Pariscraft Finger Puppet

Objectives

The combination of pariscraft and balloons results in a strong puppet. It is easy to model over the balloons and a smooth surface can be painted on pariscraft. For the lower grades, the head can be left round, and in the upper grades more relief can be developed, resulting in character study.

Again, as in the animal two-part hand puppet, these little puppets can keep a musical accompaniment merely by clapping their hands. A loud clap results, much to the delight of the audience.

Materials

Pariscraft, bowl of water, scissors, newspapers, balloons, small plastic cups to keep balloons from rolling (optional).

Procedure

- Have strips of pariscraft already cut and newspapers spread out.
- Blow up balloon and set in a shallow plastic dish.
- Begin to apply strips of pariscraft around the balloon. (Figure A) Let dry, prick balloon, and pull out. Make

A

a neck by wrapping pariscraft around the finger lightly and then securing it to the neck of the balloon, using the index finger for a model. For upper grades model features.

- Wind pariscraft around the thumb and middle finger, adding a slight flare to hold the clothes on. Now the parts are ready. (Figure B)
- The puppet can be manipulated as in Figure C.
- Make dress, add hair, paint features. (Figure D)

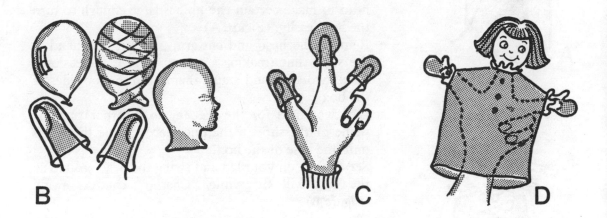

B   C   D

Lesson 7   Shoe Box Puppet

Objectives

Maybe we should call this puppet the ventriloquist's dummy, since his size and structure make him most adaptable for sitting on laps. For its easy performance and construction, this puppet is quite a show-maker. No special controls are needed and children of any age can make "Charlie" talk and move his head around.

Materials

Shoe box, brown lunch bag, strips of brown paper for arms and legs, newspaper, string, glue or stapler, crayons or paint.

Procedure

- Decide on the character and appropriate clothes for the puppet.
- Paint the bottom, sides, and top of the box as it stands in a vertical position.
- Crush newspaper and stuff the brown lunch bag. Smooth out the face part and glue yarn hair on the top only, not the sides. Tie neck.
- Cut a hole on the top side of the box and insert the head to make certain the hole is large enough to turn the head easily. (Figure A)
- Remove the head and cut arms, shaping the hand at the same time (making a mitten hand is the easiest). Make two arms and staple them onto the top sides of the box.
- Cut two strips for the feet, again incorporating the shape of the shoe in the one piece. Staple these legs onto the base of the box.
- Set the box on your lap and swing the head around so the hair will fly while "Charlie" chatters away. (Figure B)

A

B

Lesson 8   Grocery Bag Puppet

Objectives

Music is part of the elementary school curriculum where keeping time with rhythm instruments is popular. This puppet is quiet when keeping time. He looks as if he is enjoying the music while apparently sitting down for the fun. For some sound, small bells can be tied to the hands. By stuffing the bag, including a heavy lump of plasticine stapled to a cardboard base, the puppet is ready to play with at any time.

Materials

Large grocery bag, strips of other bags for arms, string, single paper or stuffed lunch bag for head, crayons or paint, stapler or glue, plasticine, cardboard.

Procedure

- Cut the arms and hands in one piece and staple or glue them to the top sides and let it set.
- Guide the children in the proportion of the head in relation to the grocery bag. Cut on heavy paper or cut double pieces and glue together. Bend the neck to make a tab and glue on top of the bag.
- On the front of the bag draw legs, but only the knees to the shoes as if he were sitting down with his knees bent. Color.
- Press lump of plasticine on a piece of cardboard, stuff with newspapers, and staple edges of the bag to the base.
- Tie strings to the hands and the puppet is eager to begin moving his arms in time with the music. (Figure A)
- Have child stand in back of this puppet to manage him.

Lesson 9   Spool Puppet

Objectives

Collecting spools is easy and a row of them sitting on a shelf can some day turn into a collection of small puppets for little children to enjoy. A variety of sizes comes in handy for different characters. All one needs is scrap paper, thread, and crayons or soft pencils for features and clothes. Not only people can be made but animals, too; once pupils begin using spools for the bodies all sorts of ideas will develop.

Materials

Variety of spools, scraps of paper, cloth or paper for clothes, waterproof glue, string.

Procedure

- Plan the size of head in proportion to the spool that will be the body.
- Use double paper for strength. Is it a boy or girl? Cut the appropriate hair and face all in one piece. Cut out, color, set aside.
- Paint the spool and decorate the clothes with buttons, etc.
- Cut arms and legs. When the spool is dry, glue in place.
- Bend the hands and feet forward for a realistic effect.
- Add a heavy thread or thin string to top of the head.
- Walk the spool puppet along to meet other friends. (Figure A)

A

Lesson 10 "Favorite Paper Doll" Puppet

Objectives

Paper dolls are available everywhere and most little girls have their own paper-doll books. They are often seen in newspapers and magazines to be cut out and played with. By mounting a favorite paper doll on heavier paper it can easily be made into a bouncing puppet. By cutting the paper doll at the waist and knees and rejoining slightly apart with bandaids, the doll will be able to sit and walk with a little guiding.

Materials

Favorite paper doll, glue, scissors, string, bandaids, heavy paper.

Procedure

- Glue the paper doll on heavy paper and cut out neatly. Let it set to dry, pressing it flat.
- Cut the doll in half at the waist. Separate the two pieces so a space of an eighth of an inch is obtained and secure a bandaid on the back.

A

B

- Do the same at the knee of each leg. (Figure A)
- Add string to the knees with a big loop and manipulate the legs with the left hand.
- Tie string to the top of the head and hold with right hand.
- Now try making her walk and sit down. (Figure B)
- If she seems a little light in weight, attach bits of cardboard to her feet, which should be bent forward to resemble real shoes.
- Let the children try ideas of their own with their favorite paper dolls.

Bonus Ideas

Talking Box Puppet

Draw features of a character in a story on the base of the box. Glue yarn on top and arrange an appropriate style of hair. Cut a slit for the mouth wide enough to slip four fingers through. Set the box puppet facing the audience. Keep fingers together but move up and down while talking.

Fist and Scarf Hand Puppet

Close the hand to form a fist. Have someone tie a scarf around the hand. Bend elbow so hand appears over the shoulder, back to audience, with the thumb knuckle facing them. Cut two white disks of paper, draw in the iris and pupil, and with a dab of paste adhere to either side of the thumb. Paint a mouth and two dots for the nostrils. Wiggle the thumb for animation. Use both fists for a two-character puppet play.

Plastic-Bag Fish Puppet

Use the small tear-off bags. Blow air into the bag and close with a rubber band a u two inches from the end. Glue large eyes and fins plus thread to op of body where it balances. Make a second fish, ecu to other en of thread, and manipulate the twins.

Twig Puppet

Find twigs with two ranches that resemble arms, about 8″ long. Cut an oval for the head and draw in features. Make a second oval of the same size for the back of the head and color for hair. Use leaves or cloth for clothes. Manipulate puppet just below table edge.

Paper-Bag Rabbit with Strings to Hop

Use any size bag and stuff lightly with newspaper. On the base of the bag draw the rabbit features. Tie two inches from the base to form the head. Close the end of the bag about an inch to form a tail. Make long ears, staple them to each side of the head, and attach a string at the pointed end of the ears. Tie a long string at each side of the hips—this makes a long loop to make the bunny hop. When the rabbit stops, drop the string for the ears and they will fall.

Jump-Out-of-the-Box Puppet

Find either a small cardboard box such as the kind earrings come in or paper baking cup box. Cut long strips of construction paper smaller than the box and fold accordion fashion. Add a flat paper head. Stuff the box, quickly open, and out jumps the puppet.

Sock Hand Puppet

Any discarded sock will do. Glue a piece of red paper on the sole, or sew on red cloth, which will last longer. Insert two small stones for the eyes and tie with thread. Insert the hand, open and close the mouth to simulate talking.

Marionette Fabric Puppet

Cut out clothes, head, arms, and legs using two patterns of each. Glue these together and let dry. Make the joints with single pieces of material so they will stay limp. Attach threads to joints and add a handle to hold threads (usually a cross piece).

Finger Walking Puppets

Either draw and color a 5" figure or cut one from a magazine, gluing it onto light cardboard. Cut two holes to insert the index and middle finger. Now walk the puppet on the table. Using both hands, two puppets can act at the same time, or dance to music.

Cardboard and Rubber Band Bird Puppet

Cut a bird out of construction paper using two patterns and glue together. Make accordion-fold wings and insert through the body; when wings are balanced add a dab of glue at the insert and let dry. Find the balance point of the body and staple the rubber band in place. Spring the bird into the air and watch it fly up and down according to the arm motion.

CHAPTER 2

Festive Baskets

*T*hroughout the school year containers are used for many purposes. They include a gamut of forms: vases, portfolios, satchels, and baskets of various construction. Baskets can be used as seasonal decorations, functional items, and gifts. The smallest containers in basket form can be used as place-card candy surprises, or the large grocery brown bag can be transformed into a handbag or tote bag.

Basket making can involve a lesson in accurate measuring and folding or freeform creative containers can tease the inventive mind of the imaginative child.

Festive baskets can be constructed from kindergarten to sixth grade with a wide range of materials and from the simplest style to more detailed, concentrated work.

Lesson 1   Paper Plate and Baking Cup Basket

Objectives

The kitchen is a gold mine of art ideas. Paper cups, paper plates, and paper baking cups challenge the imagination to produce festive baskets.

Materials

Paper plate, paper baking cups, paper drinking cup, Duco-cement, paper puncher, pipe cleaners—12″ length, pencil, ruler.

Procedure

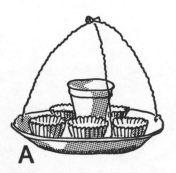

- Select a firm white paper plate with a strong, flat rim.
- Punch three holes at equal distance from each other.
- For the 4″ drinking cup find the exact center of the plate by dividing the diameter in half vertically and horizontally.
- Draw around the base of the cup for the center and apply waterproof glue. Set the drinking cup there and weight it down with a book until set.
- Select five different or alternately colored paper baking cups and plan the arrangement around the center cup. Glue them down.
- Secure the three pipe cleaners joining at the top; add a gaily colored bow. (Figure A) The basket is now a centerpiece for parties and picnics.

A

Lesson 2   Brown Lunch Bag Baskets

Objectives

The brown lunch bag so often carried to school makes a different kind of basket. The durability of the bag can be increased by the addition of Contac or self-adhesive paper, which is available in a variety of patterns.

Materials

Brown paper lunch bag, scissors, self-adhesive paper.

Procedure

- Place the bag flat on the wrong side of the self-adhesive paper. Trace around the bag carefully, cut two pieces. Do not remove the backing yet.
- Measure the side pieces and cut two.
- Stand the bag upright and trace around the base; now five pieces are ready to adhere.
- Start with the plain side of the bag first. Peel off the backing and, starting at the top, slowly seal it down.

Lift up as a wrinkle appears and reseal. Do the same to the remaining sides and bottom.

- To make a handle, open bag top flat and cut the opening. (Figure A)

A

Lesson 3   Elephant Cereal Box Basket

Objectives

Teach the child one idea and you will develop in him an interest in creating his own individual designs from double boxes.

Materials

Two small cereal boxes that fit inside each other (from the ten pack), paper puncher, ribbons, scraps of white paper, scissors, marker, paste.

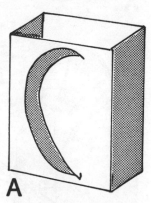

A

Procedure

- Start with the smaller cereal box. Peel off the outer wrapper leaving the inside waxed paper bag.
- Remove wrapper of larger box and draw large elephant ears on each side. (Figure A) Bend them forward.
- Draw the small eyes high up on the narrow side of the box.
- Draw the trunk on the narrow side first before cutting. Cut and curl trunk over a pencil, pasting a name tag on the inside of the curled trunk.
- Leave white, or paint or spray the box grey, or any color you wish.
- Punch side holes on the outside box and tie ribbons.
- Insert the smaller box and this jolly elephant basket is ready for party place cards. (Figure B)

B

Lesson 4   Bunny Cream Carton Basket

Objectives

The ready-made half-pint cream carton is an extremely strong item to work with. This style of box affords a young artist endless opportunities.

A

Materials

Half-pint cream container, tin can, newspaper, pipe cleaner, scraps of white paper, scissors, waterproof glue, quick-drying enamel spray paint.

Procedure

- Thoroughly rinse the carton with warm, soapy water.
- Open the spout and insert a pipe cleaner for the handle. Staple it closed. (Figure A)
- Set up a newspaper spray booth and place the carton on a shallow tin can (so it won't stick to the newspaper), and spray to cover all the advertising.
- Now add eyes, nose, whiskers, ears, front paws, and tail. (Figure B) The bunny is ready for marbles or candies.
- This same idea can be used with the school-lunch milk carton as a stand-up bunny. (Figure C)

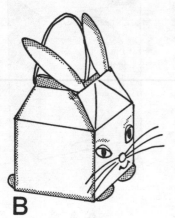

B

C

Lesson 5   Screen Stitchery Basket

Objectives

Modern window screening is ideal for stitchery. It can be purchased by the yard at hardware stores, and is soft and free from sharp edges. A simple pattern of construction paper can be the basis for a handsome and original basket.

Materials

Screening, pattern, scissors, felt or cloth for appliqué, brightly colored yarns, large blunt needle, straight pins.

Procedure

- Make a pattern of any size you choose. Follow the basic plan for making boxes. (Figure A) Cut along the short A-B lines. Fold on C-C and D-D lines and pin to hold in place to see how it looks.
- Remove pins and run a colored yarn on the four lines to establish the edges of the bag and make it easier to design the stitchery, working while it is flat.
- When the basic designs on the four sides are completed, fold the bag into position and sew around the top with an easy blanket stitch or stitch of your choice.
- Add the handles, stitching them in place. This makes an extra strong and transparent bag for many uses. (Figure B)

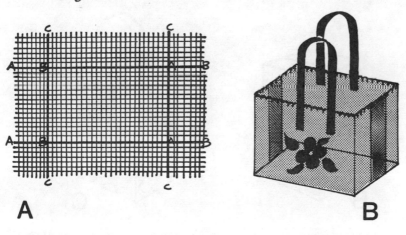

A   B

Lesson 6   Tissue Box Basket

Objectives

The variety of shapes, sizes, and colors of tissue boxes offers excellent art material. Children can bring these clean, strong containers to school to be transformed into ideal baskets for all occasions.

Materials

Tissue boxes (oval push-out part saved), pipe cleaners, quick-drying spray (optional), decorations of felt cutouts, etc.

Procedure

- Fold the oval push-out section in half. (Figure A)

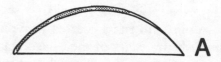

- Cut two slits in the top of the box and slip the folded ends inside. Slide the pipe cleaner through the ends and twist to hold the handle firmly. (Figure B)
- Decorate the box with felt cutouts, self-adhering paper, bands of colored Mystik tape, or use your own ideas. (Figure C)

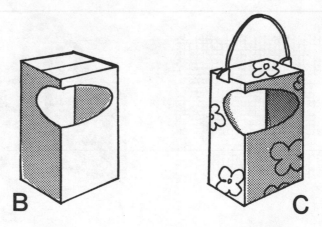

Lesson 7   Hanging Paper Plate Basket

Objectives

To use paper plates as a practical art form.

Materials

Four paper plates with flat rims, pipe cleaners, stapler, yarn, cardboard, scissors, Duco-cement, paper puncher.

Procedure

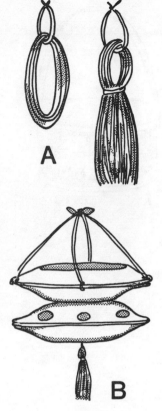

- For the top plate cut out the center circle. To avoid mistakes, make a pattern first.
- Staple the second plate rim to rim with the top one.
- On the third plate cut four or five holes on the sloping part.
- Make a tassel. Wind colored yarn around the length of cardboard where you want the tassel to be. Slip off this coiled yarn and tie a piece of yarn through the opening. Tie another knot about 1" down and finally cut the ends. (Figure A)
- Insert this tassel by securely tying the ends through a hole in the base of the fourth plate. Tape inside. Glue the fourth plate to the third and the third to the second.
- Punch holes on top rim and tie. This special basket will hold dried-flower or leaf arrangements. (Figure B)

Lesson 8   Tin Can and Pariscraft Basket

Objectives

To learn how to artistically combine discarded tin cans and art material to produce functional and attractive baskets.

Materials

Short tin can, pariscraft, marker, bowl of water, scissors, newspapers, paints of your choice, waxed paper.

Procedure

- Cut three strips of pariscraft long enough to encircle the tin can.

- Place the can on dry pariscraft and trace around it. Cut one-half inch larger and cut slits around the edge.
- Dip the circle into water and cover the base of the can. Bend the cut edge up to secure it in place. Wrap other strips around the can, making it smooth by rubbing more water into the gauze.
- Decide on the length of handle needed. Roll strips of pariscraft and bend to fit the sides. Let it dry on waxed paper and then join it to the sides with more pariscraft.
- Decorate the tin-can basket or add the party guest's name. (Figure A)

A

Lesson 9   Flat Papier-mâché Pedestal Basket

Objectives

Papier-mâché is a popular and much-used material in the upper grades, however, the flat papier-mâché version is easier to handle for younger children and has equally effective results.

Materials

Sheets of newspaper, wallpaper paste, scissors, paints, pipe cleaners, rock or plastic bowl, pan of water, waxed paper.

Procedure

- Cover working area with newspaper. Place an interestingly shaped rock or a plastic bowl on the newspaper.
- Lay a single sheet of newspaper on the covered table and brush on a layer of wallpaper paste. Continue until three layers are ready, leaving the top one free from paste.
- Cover the rock with waxed paper. If a plastic bowl is used, omit this step. Cut slits on the edges of the newspaper draped over the bowl and overlap. (Figure A)

A

- Turn upside down and trim edges folding outward, not into, the bowl. Smooth the outside with added water and paste. Let dry.
- When dry, slip off and make a second one.
- When the two are shaped and dry, glue them base to base so this basket has a pedestal.
- Add handle and decorate using a seasonal or everyday theme, being sure to camouflage the joining of the two bowls. (Figure B)

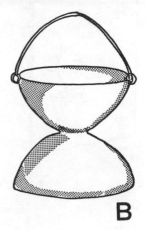

B

Lesson 10   Wall Relief Baskets

Objectives

Further experimentation with paper cups leads to other ways of using them for unusual effects. This design can be used as a wall relief or as a hanging-in-space idea.

Materials

Paper drinking cups (4" high), scissors, waterproof cement, cardboard for backing, spray paint (optional), pipe cleaner.

Procedure

- Cut three paper drinking cups in half. This will make two wall plaques of relief baskets, to be used as companion pieces.
- Practice arranging these three halves on the size cardboard you have chosen. When a pleasing design is made, trace lightly with a pencil around the half cups. Run waterproof glue on this line and on the edges of the half cups. Glue them in place. Weight them down until set.
- For added strength, when dry spray with a gold spray.
- Tack on the wall or add a pipe cleaner loop to hang it up. (Figure A)

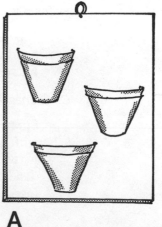

A

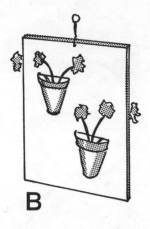

B

- To make a hanging whole-cup basket, plan design as previously described. Draw around the sides of the cups; cut at sides; put bottom on cardboard backing. Slip the cups in place and glue.
- Hang this basket up so it can revolve with autumn leaves, dried, light-weight flowers, or flowers the children made. (Figure B)

Bonus Ideas

Plastic Container Baskets

Almost any plastic container can be made into a basket. One that is practically ready to use is the small-sized margarine container, already decorated. Simply add a pipe-cleaner handle and secure a bright bow—just the right size for little hands.

Turkey Party Baskets with Cream Cartons

Rinse cream cartons with warm, soapy water and let dry. Spray with brown paint. Make several layers of cut brown paper to form a fan-shaped tail. With white paint or crayon draw in the white markings at the tips of the feathers. Add brown drooping feathers, orange feet, and head. A pipe-cleaner handle completes this party ornament that can be filled with nuts.

Paper Baking Cup Favors

Glue differently colored cups on small cardboard disks. Make two handles that cross with a bow at the top. These are gay little baskets for school or home parties.

Christmas Tree Baskets

Spray a small, round container bright red. Make a triangle handle with green pipe cleaners joining at the top with a loop. Make a pattern of a cone shape to fit inside the container resting against the handles; cover with sequins or gold stars. Fill with candy, and then insert the rolled cone shape.

Newspaper Hat Baskets

Fold the newspaper like a hat, except make it smaller. Open the hat slightly so it stands alone. Insert small lollipops in the sides. Make a one-loop paper handle.

Macramé Hanging Basket

Use a simple knot pattern in a rectangular shape. Sew the edges together or weave them with string. Stretch open and secure a tassel at the center base, and long strings, either knotted or plain, at the top for hanging. Experiment with pieces of macramé, such as wrapping it around a small tin can and adding handles.

Valentine Double Candy Basket

Any small valentine candy box can be utilized for creating baskets. Place the top upside down on the base. Use invisible tape to join together. Make a wide, red handle of stiff paper or sheets of paper glued together. Punch small holes to hold lollipops or stick candy.

Chiclet Standing Basket

Collect empty Chiclet boxes, spray with bright color, and let dry. Place them back to back and glue the two flaps together. Fill with small candies and stand basket up tent-fashion for little people's parties.

Halloween Cat Basket

Wrap a small, flat, tin can with black construction paper. Cut orange eyes, nose, and mouth and glue in place. Glue black pointed ears onto the side; add a handle.

Paper Plate Drawstring Bag

Insert a small paper plate inside a colored plastic bag, staple. Stitch top down, run a drawstring through.

CHAPTER 3

Pop Art and Op Art Jewelry

*T*he desire for self-adornment goes back to the beginnings of man. In the grade school curriculum the study of many cultures presents inspiring motivation in design, style, and color in creating jewelry.

The abbreviated names of Pop and Op art, as they are commonly called, form a part of twentieth-century art. By showing examples and explaining the artists' objectives, you can make the children aware of the roles of Pop and Op in contemporary art.

Pop art means Popular art, a term applied to work designed for the masses in which inexpensive materials are used and simple themes are easily understood. Op art means Optical art, in which the artist creates pictures that deliberately confuse the eye. Examples are everywhere—canvas that seems to move in dizzying patterns, fractions of cubes that move in space, and bubbling spots of color that boil and jump about on flat surfaces.

These artists use brilliant, clear colors and bold designs, ideal for reference and motivation in jewelry making.

Lesson 1 Plaster of Paris Pendants

Objectives

Plaster of Paris is a fascinating medium for all age groups. It does, however, demand well-organized work areas and supplies. It is well suited for creative jewelry since the material accepts paint and decorations well.

Materials

Plaster of Paris, water, newspapers, plastic spoons, paper

cups, watercolor box and brush, string, straws, sequins, waxed paper, small beads (optional).

Procedure

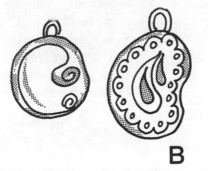

- Spread newspaper on the table and a sheet of waxed paper on top. A plain sheet of newsprint under the waxed paper is optional.
- Fill a paper cup one-third full of water. Sprinkle plaster of Paris into water but do not stir at this point.
- When a dry island remains firmly above water level, and not before, begin to stir the mixture until it is creamy smooth. Tap the cup to release air bubbles and watch them rise to the top. (Figure A)
- Cut 4" loops of string and arrange them away from each other. Short straws 2" wide can be embedded in the plaster for pendants.
- Pour the plaster over the string so a generous loop is left. Be sure the shapes are thick enough. Use up all the plaster, adding extra drippings to already set plaster for a relief effect.
- Press the jewels in and let them set. Paint and display. (Figure B)

B

Lesson 2 Flat Papier-mâché Bracelets and Pins

Objectives

Flat papier-mâché is less commonly used, yet it offers a different approach to jewelry making and can be handled easily in the lower grades. Its flat surface makes painting simple and bold designs can be created with more freedom.

Materials

Newspapers, wallpaper paste (starch can also be used), scissors, waxed paper, flat paintbrush, water, paints of your choice, gloss finish, newsprint, pin backs.

Procedure

- Spread newspaper over the work area. Cut single sheets of newspaper in half.
- Place half of a single sheet of newspaper on the table. Brush wallpaper paste over it with a wide brush. On top of this pasted paper lay a second dry sheet. Again brush over with paste. No paste is needed on the third sheet. (Figure A)
- Smooth out the three layers so they are free from wrinkles.
- Preplan your size of bracelet on newsprint. Cut it out and try it on for fit.
- Place this pattern on the flat papier-mâché and cut it out. Overlap it to join and smooth the edges. Stand it around a plastic bottle or shape it so it will dry perfectly round.
- Cut an oval, circle, or square shape for the size pin you want. Smooth the edges with paste. Crush tiny balls of pasted paper and paste in a design around the edge or however you wish.
- Let dry, paint, and add gloss finish and pin backs. (Figure B)

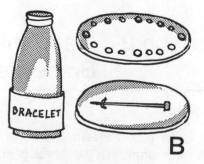

Lesson 3 Instant Papier-mâché Beads and Pins

Objectives

Instant papier-mâché is not always easily available for use in large classes, but if the opportunity arises it is a good experience. Actually it is an "instant" version of paper pulp, which is time consuming to prepare, hence one has all the many advantages this newer product offers.

Materials

A package of Instant Papier-Mâché, plastic bowl, water, waxed paper, string, tempera paints, gloss finish, acrylics (optional), knitting needle, the size of which depends on your choice.

Procedure

- Place a sheet of newspaper on the table and cover it with waxed paper.
- Mix the Instant Papier-Mâché as directed on the package. Use a plastic bowl it makes cleanup easier.
- When of correct consistency, roll the size of the bead you want between your hands and pierce it with a knitting needle. Dip your fingers in water and smooth the outside. Make as many as you need of different sizes. (Figure A)
- When they are dry, paint them individually on a knitting needle and transfer to another needle to set aside to dry again.
- To apply the gloss, thread each bead separately with string and dip in material, put back on needle to dry.
- Pins can be made by shaping petals. Place on a flat backing.

A

Lesson 4 Sawdust and Wallpaper Paste Beads and Pins

Objectives

This is one of the least expensive ways to make strong, durable jewelry in school. It produces an interesting texture that can be emphasized or smoothed out; it is light in weight, and can be spray painted or decorated by hand.

Materials

Sawdust, wallpaper paste, plastic bowl, waxed paper, plastic spoons, newspapers, string, knitting needles, small cup of flour.

Procedure

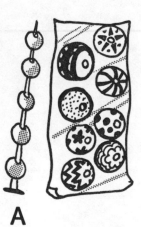

A

- Prepare the wallpaper paste. There is one on the market that will not ferment and lasts for months once it is prepared and stored in plastic or glass containers.
- Mix in the desired amount of sawdust and stir thoroughly.
- Dust your hands with a small amount of flour and roll a spoonful around between them. Pierce the ball on a knitting needle to make the size hole you want for threading.
- Place these balls on waxed paper or let dry on extra needles.
- Spray paint or paint by hand. (Figure A)

Lesson 5 Pariscraft Bracelets, Pendants, and Rings

Objectives

The artist George Segal has promoted pariscraft into acceptance as an art form and it is popular in the art programs of today. It is especially good for jewelry because of its quick-hardening quality, easily painted smooth surface, and permanence.

Materials

Pariscraft, water, scissors, newspapers, waxed paper, oaktag, string or yarn, suitable "jewel" from an old pin.

Procedure

- Starting with the bracelet, cut a pattern from oaktag or lightweight cardboard. Determine the width and length needed to slip it over the hand. Staple it for the size.
- Cut strips of pariscraft and begin to cover the pattern, smoothing out any wrinkles around the form. Do not lose the symmetry of the circle, at least for the first one.
- Dip fingers in water frequently to move the plaster around in the gauze; this provides a smooth surface on which to paint.
- Let it dry and paint bold Op art designs on it. Finish with a coat of gloss or varnish. A second bracelet can have relief designs.
- Cut a pattern for the pendant. Make a loop at the top of pariscraft and cover; this time make a rim in the center to embed a jewel from an old pin. Design a matching ring using the same method. (Figure A)

A

Lesson 6   Fabric and Payon Belt with Pariscraft Buckle

Objectives

Here is a combination of three materials that blend well together to make a practical belt. It provides an opportunity to use either Pop or Op art and the small amount of pariscraft needed for the belt will give every child a chance to experience this lesson.

Materials

Fabric (preferably old sheeting), Payons, water, bowl, oaktag, scissors, pariscraft, water.

Procedure

- Let the child measure his waist to determine the belt's length and width. Double this width so it can be folded over.
- For motivation, study American Indian, Egyptian, and other designs and draw the general idea on scrap paper.
- With newspaper underneath and an extra sheet of newsprint on top so the cloth will not pick up the print, dip the cloth in water and place on the newsprint. Begin drawing with Payons to create your design, but plan it in the center. (Figure A)
- When dry, fold so seam is in the middle. Glue it with waterproof glue or let the child take it home to be stitched, closing it at the ends.
- Make the buckle by cutting an oaktag pattern. Cover it with pariscraft. There need not be a set way to cover the buckle frame as long as it is smooth and free from wrinkles. (Figure B)
- When the belt is stitched and dry, join to buckle through the center division and tack in place.

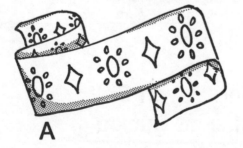

A

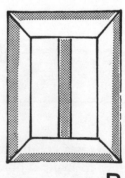

B

Lesson 7   Macramé Necklace

Objectives

Macramé is a recently popularized art form that increases skills in creating knots of all sizes and construction. Once the basic instruction is given, the child can create his own innovations.

Materials

Yarn, heavy string, masking tape, scissors, cord.

Procedure

- Cut two pieces of heavy yarn, each a yard long. After practice you may decide more knots are wanted, hence more yarn length.
- Find the center and tie a knot. Tape this at the top of the table. Begin about 12″ down and tie your first square knot. (Figure A) Use tape to hold yarn above knot.

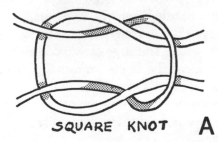

SQUARE KNOT   A

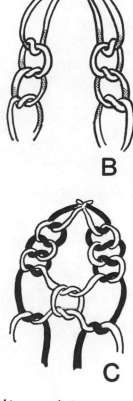

B

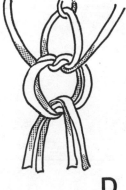

C

D

- Leave an inch space and make another square knot, three in all.
- Do the same to the other side. (Figure B)
- Join the two inside lines in another square knot. Then join the two outside lines to those on the inside. (Figure C)
- Now make plain knots the same way each time and watch this part turn. Make a final knot with double strands and trim. (Figure D)

Lesson 8   Mexican Pottery or Marblex Jewelry Set

Objectives

Since jewelry takes such a small amount of material, the rich terra-cotta color of Mexican pottery actually needs no additional color other than possibly a gloss finish, but this is optional.

Materials

Mexican pottery or Marblex, water, newspapers, flour, waxed paper, knitting needles, string, gloss finish (optional), dull knife, safety pin.

Procedure

- Mix the Marblex or Mexican pottery as directed on the package. Spread newspapers on work table and cover with waxed paper to prevent clay from sticking.
- Scoop out enough for the size bead needed. Flour your hands and roll bead between palms; pierce on knitting needle. Transfer to a smaller needle so beads can dry. Plan a variety of bead sizes, small to large, large to small, and urge creative ideas.
- Either leave the bead smooth or pierce the outside with a design. (Figure A)
- Roll a coil around the finger designated for a ring and flatten for comfort. Use same pierced design as beads. (Figure B)

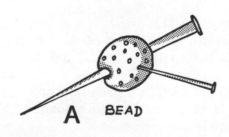

A   BEAD

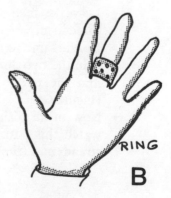

RING

B

- Make a bracelet to match. Roll coil around arm so it can be slipped over the hand easily. Flatten and pierce designs to complete the set.
- Jewelry can be painted, but don't overlook the beauty of the natural color, too.

Lesson 9 Cotton Mesh Stitchery Collar

Objectives

Here is another use for stitchery with brilliant Pop art ideas. Collars like this can actually be used on clothes, or they can be designed to resemble historical garb and worn with costumes.

Materials

Sheeting or paper for pattern, brilliantly colored yarns, scissors, blunt needle, ribbons (optional).

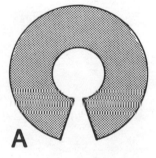

Procedure

- Plan the collar by making a pattern of either paper or old sheeting. (Figure A)
- With crayon, develop a general idea of color contrast.
- Cut pictures from magazines of eyes, fruits, and single clear, bright objects. Glue them on the mesh and stitch yarn designs around them. This makes a Pop art collar. A beanie could be made the same way. (Figure B)
- Edge the collar with a strong stitch, such as the easy blanket stitch, in contrasting colors. Add in-and-out weaving for borders and include ideas the children will be creating.
- Tie the collar either in front or in back. Use bright ribbons or matching yarns.

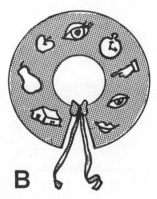

Lesson 10 Pipe Cleaner, Paper Clip, and Yarn Necklace

Objectives

What an excellent chance to make a necklace out of classroom materials! A little start will open avenues of new ideas for the children to create.

Materials

Paper clips, pipe cleaners, yarns, scissors.

Procedure

- Proceed to join the paper clips until the length is right for you.
- Make a circle out of the pipe cleaner and join by twisting.
- Make a small loop at the top of the circle.
- Using the reverse double half hitch knot, make several on the circle with different colored yarns. (Figure A)
- Add to the circle as far as you like with the colored yarns or reverse the double half hitch knot. (Figure B)

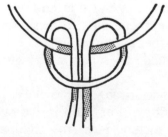

REVERSE DOUBLE HALF HITCH

A

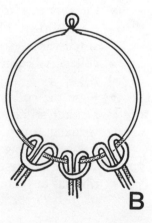

B

- In place of a paper clip necklace make a heavy, braided yarn chain. (Figure C)

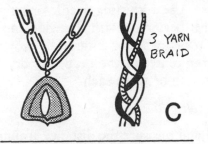

Bonus Ideas

Necklace of Buttons and Felt Scraps

Resort to the collage box of scraps in the classroom for all kinds of jewelry. Plan the necklace on the table alternately using buttons and colored felt scraps. Then string them with the felt between the buttons.

Tissue and Pipe Cleaner Tiaras or Crowns

Costumes often call for crowns and those made of pipe cleaners are perfect for the short duration of their use. Twist the pipe cleaners together to make a circle to fit the pupil wearing it. Make your own original design of height, covering the back with colored tissue paper.

Tooled Pendants

Cut a piece of cardboard into the size and shape needed. Cover with two layers of foil and punch a hole at the top. With a dull end of a pencil depress a series of dots around the edge, continuing with a variety of curved and radial lines. Add braided yarn for the chain or just use plain string.

Yarn and Pipe Cleaner Bracelet

Make a circle of pipe cleaner to slip over the hand. Braid yarn around this with three different colors, ending with a short tassel.

Dog Collars with Ribbon and Sequins

Place a 1″ ribbon around the neck and mark where it meets. Allow enough ribbon to tie in the back or use snaps. Plan a design of colorful sequins or small buttons, then glue to ribbon.

Magazine Page Beads

Select a bright, colorful magazine page and cut 6″ long triangles 2″ wide at the base. Use a knitting needle or long pencil and wrap the triangle around it beginning with the wide end. Then brush paste on the rest of the paper, winding it carefully around the pencil until the point ends in the center of the bead. Let dry and thread, placing a small bead or button between each.

String and Starch Jewelry

Close the hand and measure the distance around. Select a tin can the same size, and wrap it with waxed paper. Dip string into starch or thick wallpaper paste and plan a design of lines around the can. Let it dry, remove, and spray paint for both color and support. Rings and other jewelry can be made this way.

Paper Contac Rings and Bracelets

Contac comes in a wide range of colors and patterns; the stained-glass pattern, bright and beautiful, is fine for gifts. First make patterns from any drawing paper. Then cut the Contac paper making two patterns of each, since these are to be adhered together for front and back. A narrow strip of construction paper could be added in the center for stiffening.

Headbands from Onion Bags

Headbands and belts are easily made by weaving onion bags cut into the width and length needed. Use bright yarns.

Macaroni Jewelry

The macaroni section in the grocery store is a potential jewelry store. Experiment with gluing them on pendants, or, after softening in hot water, string them in beautiful necklaces. Spray paint.

CHAPTER 4

Jovial Birds

*T*he creation of birds in art class is not only fascinating, but knowledge-increasing as well. Nature is perhaps the best place to discover design, color, line, symmetry, and other basic elements of art. Bird camouflage, a study in itself, can also be included in this unit because of its relevance to the bird's beauty.

Realistic and fun birds in jovial moods are presented here to fit the needs of classroom curriculum.

Lesson 1   Clothespin Birds and Birdbath

Objectives

To become acquainted with color by making a toy for small children and as a lesson in color theory for older children.

Materials

Paper plate, paper cup, six clip-style clothespins, Duco-cement, blue construction paper, colored scrap paper for the birds, scissors, black crayon.

A

Procedure

- Practice drawing birds using a circle for the head, an oval for the body, and a narrow oval for the tail. (Figure A)
- Add a rectangular shape under the bird for a tab.
- Cut six birds out of the following colored papers: red, yellow, blue, orange, green, and violet. Be sure the

birds are one inch shorter than the clothespin for easy handling. Fold the tab and glue the bird onto one of the colored papers. (Figure B) Do this with each bird.

- Cut a circle of blue construction paper to fit the inside recessed area of the paper plate; this represents the water. Glue it in place. (Figure C)
- Turn the plate upside down and glue a paper cup in the center. (Figure D) Place a heavy book over the cup to weight it down, leaving it for a while to allow the glue to set.
- When dry, stand the birdbath upright and clip the colored birds around the edge. (Figure E)
- To teach color theory, play a game. Let the cool-colored birds—blue, green, and purple—fly away. Leave the warm-colored birds—red, yellow, and orange—in place.

B

C

D

E

Lesson 2   Paper Sculpture Owl

Objectives

Changing a flat piece of paper into a three-dimensional form has definite appeal to children. Sometimes a teacher can supply precut paper of a special size for a project. This is one area where it would be helpful, since the cutting is a simple procedure. This owl can be individually mounted on a paper plate as suggested here or stapled to a bulletin board that has been decorated with natural branches and autumn leaves.

Materials

Paper plate (round or oval), black construction paper, black crayon, two brass fasteners, scraps of orange paper, paste, scissors, thin branch, 4" x 6" white rectangle, white 4" triangular paper.

Procedure

- Cut a black circle to fit the inside of a paper plate. Paste it down.
- Hold a precut rectangular shape of white paper vertically; fold forward one-third of the way.
- At this fold cut to shape a neck, and also round off the lower corners. (Figure A)
- Draw two big eyes just above the fold, making large black pupils.
- Draw V-shaped little feathers down the front and long feathers on the sides. (Figure B)
- Take the precut white triangle that fits the top third and shape a beak of orange scrap paper. Glue this under the point. When dry, curl under for a three-dimensional look. (Figure C 1 and 2.)
- Cut two feet from orange scrap paper, curl both over a pencil and glue to the bottom of the rectangle.
- Center the owl on the black background glued to the paper plate. Push the point of the scissors through the center of the eye, push a brass fastener through, and spread open in back. Repeat with the other eye.
- Push the body of the owl up until it puffs out and staple the lower edge onto the plate.
- Glue a short branch to the plate so the owl's feet curl over the branches for realistic effect.
- Curl the dry triangle with beak glued on over a pencil. Glue only the top edge to the top of the rectangle. The owl is ready to be placed on the bulletin board to watch the class. (Figure D)

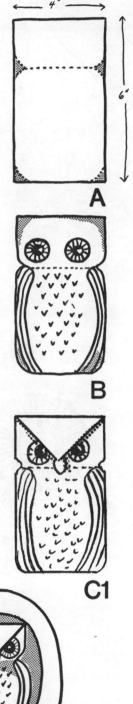

A

B

C1

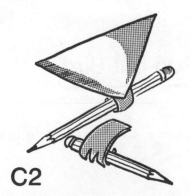

C2

D

Lesson 3   Baking Cup Birds

Objectives

Here is an easy way to make twenty-two small birds from one package of paper baking cups. These birds display soft pastel shades and are so light in weight that they can move in the air with the slightest breeze. They can rest on real branches or alight on a paper-plate bird bath.

Materials

For each bird: four paper baking cups, stapler, thread, branch or bird bath, scissors, marker.

Procedure

- For the body of the bird smooth out and flatten one paper baking cup and fold it in half. (Figure A)
- Take the folded cup and, working from the back, shape a head, beak, and tail. (Figure B)
- Fold three paper baking cups into quarters. Holding a wing on either side of the body, staple in place. Do the same with the tail. Secure a thread and hang the mobile birds. (Figure C)

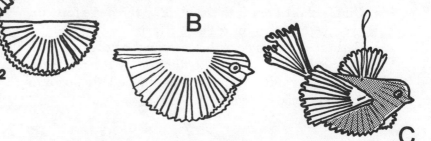

Lesson 4   Pop-out Bird

Objectives

The main objective is to teach children how to design and invent their own toys.

Materials

Small box with a flap or lift-off top (the size of paper baking-cup box is good), scissors, ruler, glue, scrap of colored paper for bird, construction paper for accordion-folded strip, picture wire or any other firm wire.

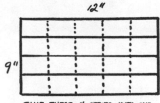

GLUE THESE 4 STRIPS INTO ONE
48" LENGTH THEN ACCORDION FOLD

Procedure

- Using the paper baking-cup box as a model, cut a 9" x 12" piece of construction paper into four strips. Mark off five folding lines. Cut the strips and tape together to make a strip 48" long. Accordion fold this strip. (Figure A)
- Draw a bird a little smaller than the width of the strip, leaving a tab that is folded back.
- When the strip of paper is accordion folded, glue the bird on the top, and the coiled wire at the bottom. (Figure B)
- Push the folded strip of paper into the box, and, gently lowering the bird, close the cover. Open quickly and watch the bird pop out. (Figure C)

B

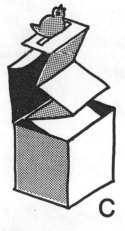

C

Lesson 5   Giant Swan to Sit In

Objectives

The swan is an ideal bird to use for this giant project. It also affords an interesting study of its habitat, environment, and characteristics. Such a project involves planned activity, cooperation in working in teams, sharing of materials, and equal effort in cleanup.

Materials

Pictures of swans for resources, newspaper, large cardboard cartons, wallpaper paste, string, torn newspapers or pariscraft, water, aprons, scissors, white water-soluble house paint, large, flat house brushes.

Procedure

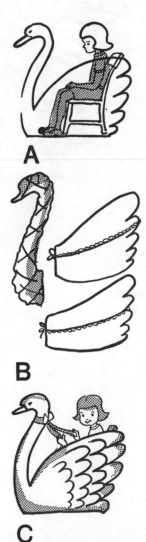

A

B

C

- Ask an average-sized child to sit on a chair to be used to measure the height of the swan. (Figure A)
- Out of newspaper cut the neck, head, and wing patterns.
- Place these on flat opened cartons, and cut patterns. You need one neck and two wings.
- With crushed newspaper, wrap around the head and neck and tie with string; pull it tight to make this part firm and strong. (Figure B) In this illustration notice that the wings are sponged with water and curved. Tie with string to hold this form.
- Decide whether you plan to use pariscraft or newspaper strips dipped in wallpaper paste. Then cover the head and neck making a smooth surface. Let dry.
- Untie the string, shape the wings, and paint white with water-soluble house paint. Retie with the string to retain the curved wings.
- With strips of pariscraft or newspaper join the neck and two wings; re-enforce strongly. When dry, paint neck and head white.
- When thoroughly dry, paint an orange bill and dark eyes.
- With light-blue paint or crayons outline feathers on the wings, drawing them away from the neck in graceful lines.
- Finally, for decoration and fun, add a wide, pink ribbon around the neck. Add narrow streamers of ribbon for reins. (Figure C)
- As a final suggestion, be sure the base of the swan is smooth so it will not scratch the floor when it is

moved. Actually, once the place for the swan has been settled on, the only part to move is the chair, which the child pulls in with him as he walks between the wings.

Lesson 6   Flat Papier-mâché Birds

Objectives

While flat papier-mâché is not as popular as the crushed version, it offers a simple way of creating the illusion of movement and action in birds both in flight and at rest. It is worth experimenting with.

Materials

Newspapers, wallpaper paste, wide, flat brush, sponge, scissors, poster or spray paints.

Procedure

- Have a generous supply of bird pictures around the room. Discuss their shapes, proportions, color, etc.
- Plan a simple pose in flight. (Figure A)

A

- Spread newspaper on a table a little larger than the pattern you decided on. Brush the first sheet of newspaper with paste; add a second sheet and repeat. Use three sheets in all.
- Smooth out the ripples created by the layers of newspapers and paste. Then cut out the pattern.

B

- Immediately shape the flat bird into a position of flight. Experiment with it. When a pose pleases you, prop it into the pose by using balls of newspaper. (Figure B) When dry, rest on a branch and glue in place.
- For a standing bird, draw a double image as shown in Figure C. Place this pattern on the newspaper and repeat the above steps. Cut into the neck and tail, bending the head down and tail up. Spread the legs, bend the feet to balance, and let dry and harden. (Figure D)

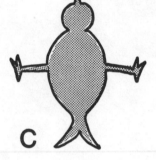

C

D

Lesson 7   Double Windmill Birds

Objectives

Sometimes it is interesting to combine an old idea with a newer one. In this case the old windmill favorite can be combined with a bird form to make wings in motion. Here the children can use different color combinations and a variety of shapes and sizes to make their own action toy.

Materials

Ruler; 9″ x 12″ white drawing paper; pencil; scissors; long, slender, thin brads; 12″ dowel post (one-quarter inch is thick enough), a sturdy, thin branch is just as good as a dowel post; two small beads or buttons; Duco-cement.

Procedure

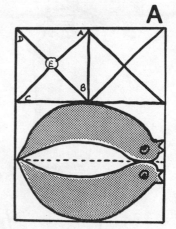

A

- One sheet of 9″ x 12″ white paper will make a double body for the birds as well as two windmills, each 4½″ wide.
- Lay out the paper as illustrated in Figure A. A simple form of a bird is better than a fancy one.
- Cut out the two birds and set aside. Make the windmills by bringing corners A, B, C, and D to the center. (Figure B) Secure and hold in place with a straight pin stuck into an eraser.
- Glue the two birds on either side of the branch. Let it set. (Figure C)
- Gently hammer the windmill into the branch or dowel post with the thin brad, but first slip in a bead or button to ease the twirling. Do the same to the other side, but nail a little lower. The bird is ready for double action. (Figure D)

B

C

D

Lesson 8   Plastic Bottle Penguin

Objectives

Exercising childrens' imaginations is good motivation for art projects in the classroom. The variety of plastic containers on the market, if saved after use, can make ideal birds of all kinds. One of the easiest is the proud penguin.

Materials

Plastic bottle, sheets of newspaper and newspaper strips, wallpaper paste, string, two small empty spools, water, scissors, poster paint. Spray varnish or any protective coating is excellent for longer duration.

Procedure

- Study photographs of penguins to understand their outstanding characteristics: flat back, puffed out stomach, etc.
- Crush a small ball of newspaper and push it into the opening of the bottle. Twist a long beak out of newspaper and tie with string to the head. (Figure A)
- With strips of newspaper dipped in wallpaper paste, secure the two small spools for feet. Let this set until dry. While drying, fold newspaper into webbed feet and glue in place. (Figure B)
- When feet and legs are firm and dry, begin to shape the body. Crush newspaper for the stomach and tie with string. For the back and wings, fold newspaper in three layers and wrap around the body, shaping the wings at the sides. Make them bend out. Add the tail, making it touch the floor to steady the penguin. (Figure C)

Lesson 9   Lunch Bag Turkey

Objectives

An inexpensive, yet festive turkey can be easily made from an ordinary brown lunch bag. They can be used as room decorations, table centerpieces for home, or even as place cards. These turkeys can be expanded in decoration from the simplest to the most ornate, depending on the age level of the pupils.

Materials

Brown lunch bags with square bases, scissors, crayons, scraps of brown paper bags, glue, scraps of brown and orange paper, sand (optional) to weight the bird down, newspapers, pictures of turkeys.

Procedure

- Place the folded bag flat on the table. Completely cover it with long orange, black, and brown crayon strokes. Turn the bag over and repeat; open the side folds and color the same way.
- With the bag still closed, fringe the open half with half-inch widths. (Figure A)
- Crush a single sheet of newspaper into a ball and stuff into the square base of the bag. Push in the four corners with your fingers to round them off. Tie with string or a rubber band at the halfway point. (Figure B)

A B C

- In this project, patterns for head and neck plus the side wings would be helpful. Or, invite the children to make their own. If patterns are needed, make the head and neck the length of the base, holding it the tall way. (Figure C) Add a tab to paste the head onto the bag.
- The head and neck can be made out of scraps of brown bags. Or they can be cut from red construction paper. Make the drooping wings from brown construction paper.
- Glue these in place as illustrated in Figure D. Push up the tail feathers.

D

- Add orange feet; since the turkey will stand up by itself, these are merely for authenticity.
- If a weighted turkey is preferred, fill a plastic bag with sand and insert in the bag. This settles the bird if it is to be used for a centerpiece, where moving of dishes might disturb him.
- If the turkey will be used as a place card, simply cut a small white paper tag, write the name of the guest on it and slip in the turkey's beak by making a short cut. Tape in place.

Lesson 10 Fantasy Coat Hanger and Nylon Bird

Objectives

Sometimes it's fun not to have to draw realistically, but rather to explore the world of fantasy. Coat hangers and old nylons provide much opportunity for creating unusual birds.

Materials

Easy-to-bend coat hangers, old nylons, scissors, thread, scraps of black or colored construction paper, stapler, glue, sequins for extra glitter (optional).

Procedure

- Children can begin this project in two ways. They can either make all kinds of drawings of birds, or they can begin with a coat hanger, bending it into a shape that pleases them.
- For this special bird, the coat hanger was stretched out to make a long bird in flight. (Figure A)
- It was then covered with a nylon stocking by pushing the hook into the toe of the nylon. It was then tied with a thread. The end was tied into a knot and the extra stocking cut off. (Figure B)

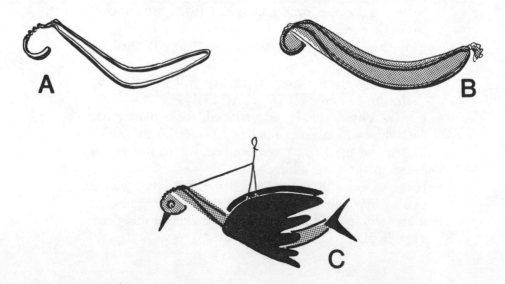

A

B

C

- The beak, eyes, and wings were then made. The wings were made from one sheet of paper and stapled onto the nylon past the wire. The tail was made from a left-over scrap of paper. The finished bird is ready to tie thread in three places to balance the bird, which will challenge the children to find the balance point. (Figure C)

Bonus Ideas

Repoussé Bird Plaques

Use heavy foil instead of copper. Cover cardboard shape with thin layer of plasticine. Place tracing of bird on top and trace lightly. With a blunt tool depress lines following feather contours. Mount and hang up.

Wire Contour Birds

Study the shape and outline of a bird carefully. Draw on paper. Place wire on top and shape bird. Place colored tissue on back of outline and glue or use as mobiles and suspend in the air.

Pipe Cleaner and Plastic Bag Birds

The small plastic tear-off bags are easy to obtain and you can make many birds from them. Blow into bag and close end, leaving enough plastic for a tail. Tie with plastic and wire pieces that come with the bags. Holding the bird vertically, glue on beak and two wings. Suspend with thread and glue in place.

Scrap Wood and Toothpick Birds

Study shapes of wood scraps and decide on a special bird or make an imaginary one. Add toothpicks to simulate feathers. Paint by hand using realistic colors of a particular bird or gay patterns of your own. Mount on a block of wood.

Balloon Birds

Blow up a variety of colored balloons of different shapes. Make up your own bird and give it a name. Glue on wings as if in flight, and suspend as a large mobile.

Calico Stuffed Birds

Cut two identical bird patterns and glue with waterproof glue, leaving an opening for newspaper stuffing. Use gaily colored fabric.

Twist double pipe cleaners for legs and make wide feet for bird to balance on. Push into body, and stand him up. Add another fabric for wings and beak.

Stitchery Bird Panel

The flexible window screening is ideal for stitchery. Draw a bird on paper in clear outline, place it under the screen, and make a running stitch to outline the bird. Fill in with brightly colored yarn either realistically or imaginatively. Mount on brightly colored paper for bulletin board displays.

Mosaic Birds

Decide on the bird to be drawn, select colored paper for bird feathers, and cut them in short, wide pieces. Fill in the body, leaving a space between mosaic pieces.

Accordion-Fold Birds

Glue two cut-out birds together, except for the tail part; separate ends. Cut paper for wings and accordion fold them, stapling them to either side of the bird. Add pipe-cleaner legs and feet if display calls for it. Otherwise staple onto branches.

Collage Birds

Plan a tall panel of heavy cardboard or use a section of the bulletin board. Have several children work together to make a composite panel. All kinds of material can be used to stimulate their imagination: real feathers, fabric, buttons, beads, yarns, string, and so on.

CHAPTER 5

Masquerade Masks

Children never cease to delight in mask-making. There are endless opportunities for this art activity. Lessons in design and color can be involved in making masks, while a social studies class might delve into the research of different cultures. Classroom plays can be enriched through mask-making, both in the art form itself and through their manipulation and use.

Finally, mask-making can be just plain fun for parties and Halloween activities.

Lesson 1 Sectional Paper Sculpture Masks

Objectives

Here is a mask that is comfortable to wear—the masquerader can eat, breath easily, speak, and yet be hidden from recognition. Its construction involves the basic principles of paper sculpture. Each part is taped to the face with invisible transparent tape.

Materials

One sheet of black 12" x 18" paper, one sheet of 9" x 12" black paper, scissors, ruler, pencil, invisible transparent tape.

Procedure

- Fold one end of the 12" x 18" paper to form a square. Cut two four-inch squares from the other end.

In between cut four or five 1/2" long whiskers. (Figure A)

- Cut the large square as illustrated in Figure A. Staple the overlapping parts. Cut the ears, cutting in on the curved edge to shape the ear.
- When the top part of the head has been stapled, glue the ears on by folding the tabs inside or tape them to the hat part. (Figure B)

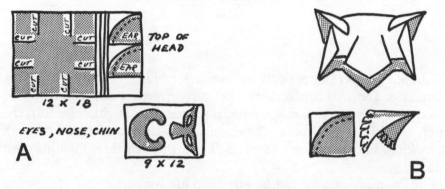

- Take the 9" x 12" black paper and cut a half mask including the nose across the 9" width. To cut the lower part, hold the paper to your face and draw how high around the mouth you want and how deep under the chin. Shapes are illustrated in Figure C.
- Add the whiskers by first curling and then gluing in place. Tape the parts to the face. (Figure D)
- Wear a black turtle-neck sweater and be a cat on Halloween.

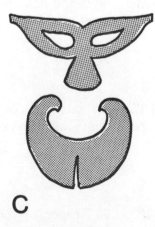

Lesson 2 Paper Bag Hood and Half Mask

Objectives

The best ideas of costuming in past history often can be used in present-day dress up. This seventeenth-century "Domino" has been simplified for inexpensive construction.

Materials

Large grocery bag, scissors, stapler, tape (if needed).

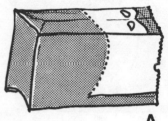

A

Procedure

- Measure the distance from the back of your head to the end of your nose.
- Placing the bag folded and flat on the table, mark this measurement from the base or back of the bag to the measurement needed, and shape the side of the hood. (Figure A)
- Leave 1" streamers and cut the rest of the sides and top.
- Completely remove the narrow underside of the bag. (Figure B)
- Using one side of the bag, measure from the top of the head to above the nose. Plan a half mask that fits you. (Figure C 1)
- Tape or glue this half mask inside the bag at the top of the head; cut out the eyes. It is ready to wear. (Figure C 2)

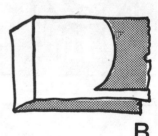

B

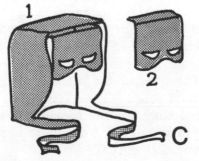

C

- Either spray the whole hood and mask or leave it the natural color and add decorations of your choice.

Lesson 3 Wall Relief Masks of Found Materials

Objectives

Numerous left-over items, such as bits of lace, yarn, rickrack braid, string, toothpicks, and so on, can be transformed into appealing wall relief masks.

Materials

Basic cardboard backing for head, cloth, yarn, toothpicks, pipe cleaners, burlap, preserve jar rubber rings, bottle caps, plastic spoons, marker, black velvet, yellow cellophane, etc.

Procedure

A

B

C

- Decide on the total size of the background. On light-weight cardboard, design the size and shape of the head.
- The mask in Figure A was painted white and then dried. Pipe cleaners were used for the hair, bottle caps for the eyes, an inverted plastic spoon for the nose, a rubber ring for the mouth, and one ring cut in half for the ears. A bow was made from scrap cloth.
- The clown's head began with the same step and then its features were built up. (Figure B) Here buttons were used for the eyes, half a rubber ball for the nose, red yarn for the mouth, toothpicks for the hair, burlap and an artificial flower for the hat, and folded white paper for the ruffle on his neck.
- The head of the cat was designed and covered with black velvet. Yellow cellophane was used for the eyes, red cloth for the tongue and strips of paper for the whiskers. Mount on white background with a black frame. (Figure C)

Lesson 4   Window Screening
Mask with Stitchery

Objectives

Present-day window screening is soft and pliable, easy and pleasant to work with, and cannot scratch or cut. Because of these qualities, it makes an excellent mask to decorate with brightly colored stitches. Children can be entirely creative and undirected with this project. Some pupils will automatically concentrate on the eyes and mouth as a design area, which is shown in this chapter. This mask is light-weight and comfortable to wear.

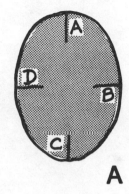

A

Materials

Window screening (plastic kind) bought by the yard in the hardware store, scissors, blunt needle, yarn or embroidery floss.

Procedure

- Cut a large oval about 10″ x 12″ in size. Cut in 3″ lengths at points A, B, C, D. (Figure A)
- Overlap these cuts to make a shell to fit the face. (Figure B)
- Holding the shell to the face position, cut out the eyes and mouth. The nose need not be cut out. It will now look like a fencing mask. Decorate with brightly colored stitchery, in this case sunbursts. (Figure C)
- For any extra-fancy ideas, cut strips of colored paper and attach them to the mask for fish or animal themes. (Figure C)

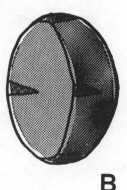

B

C

Lesson 5 Payon Cloth Masks

Objectives

Water-soluble Payons have far better results on cloth than they do on wet paper. Here again is a soft, comfortable mask for all children to enjoy, especially when they have designed it themselves. The three basic masks—half face, whole face, and pillow head—can make Halloween parties fun and original. You can award prizes for the most unusual, most funny, and others.

Materials

Old sheets are excellent for this project, water, Payons, newspapers, stapler or tacks, board, scissors.

Procedure

- An old drawing board or piece of plywood are ideal places to stretch out the material and leave it in place to dry. However, if they are not available, place several layers of newspapers on the table. Starting with the half-mask style, measure the size of mask allowing more material than needed. Position the eyes, drawing lightly with dry payon first. Wet the cloth and stretch it on the newspaper. Tack it down, put weights on the corners, or staple it to a paper pad. (Figure A)

A

- While the cloth is wet, draw in your original designs. Notice how easy it is to draw on the damp cloth and how brilliant the colors are. Let it dry, shape it, and cut out the eyes.

- Do the same for the full-face mask. Design, dry, and cut out eyes, nose, and mouth. Add strings to tie. (Figure B)
- For the pillow head mask, slide a layer of newspaper into the pillow. Wet the pillow and proceed with your ideas. Here are two to start you off. (Figure C)

B

C

Lesson 6 Half Mask with Built-In Eyelashes

Objectives

You can develop a three-dimensional mask from a single sheet of paper. A simple way to construct a half mask with one sheet of 9″ x 12″ colored paper is by folding and cutting it in such a way as to form eyelashes. Or, turn it upside down for a cat mask.

Materials

A sheet of 9″ x 12″ white or colored paper, scissors, crayons, string for ties.

Procedure

- Hold the paper horizontally and divide in half. Hold the paper to the face to locate the eyes. Draw oval eyes, nose, and cheeks. (Figure A) Always color before cutting out.
- In the top half cut a V shape in the center to help curve the paper. Then fringe the rest of the edge and bend forward. To curve eyelashes, curl upward over a pencil. (Figure B)

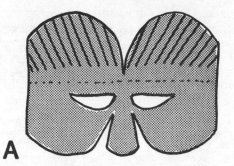

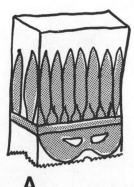

- For another way to wear the mask and to suggest a cat mask, simply turn it upside down and instead of fringing the edge, make an accordion fold. Staple it in the center. (Figure C)
- Punch holes and tie a string long enough to keep the mask on the head.

Lesson 7   Indian Headdress Mask

Objectives

Here is an American Indian theme that could possibly be used in conjunction with social studies. The study of color and design used by the American Indians affords a wide variety of ideas for costume-making, and particularly for Indian headdress masks. If the mask is not needed, it can simply be folded up in back of the front feathers.

Materials

A large grocery bag, crayons or paint, scissors.

Procedure

- Place the closed bag vertically on the table.
- Measure about four inches from the open end and draw a line around the bag. Draw another line an inch above for the headband. Position the eyes and shape the lower curve over the cheeks. (Figure A)
- Draw the feathers about 10″ high in front, sides, and back.

- The feathers in front of the bag are kept intact and not cut separately, which gives them support to stand up. However, do color them.
- The feathers beginning at the sides are cut separately all around. Fold all these feathers down over the headband and color the side that shows. Cut the headband in center and back, and overlap the band until it fits the child's head. Then staple it in place. (Figure B)
- If the mask is not needed, merely fold it back under the feathers.

B

Lesson 8   Wig and Mask from Grocery Bag

Objectives

A quick change is often needed in a school play, one that does not involve expense due to the short duration of the costume. This wig and mask combination might prove either helpful or fun during parties and plays.

Materials

Large grocery bag, glue, scissors, crayons or paint.

Procedure

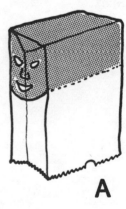

A

- Place the grocery bag flat and closed on the table. Open only one side; fold and flatten it. Measure down from the top of the child's head to his eyes and make a mark. Establish the width of the eyes (about four inches). Draw ovals for eyes, a U-shaped cut for the nose, and a mouth. Cut these out. (Figure A)
- Decide on the length for the face and cut off the bag all around. Save this.
- Measure in about 4″ at the back of the bag and draw a line on two sides of the top. Cut on this line and slide the narrow part into the front part; glue or staple in place. (Figure B)

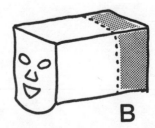

B

- Poke in the two front corners with your fingers to take square look from forehead.
- With the left-over part of the bag make fringe for the hair. (Figure C) Curl ends over a pencil and design your own wig. Bangs are good for this wig and mask combination. (Figure D)
- If colored hair is needed, spray it first before gluing it in place, or color it with crayons.

C

D

Lesson 9   TV Dinner Tray Mask

Objectives

Instead of discarding containers, the experienced teacher has learned to study their potential first. It is good to acquaint the children with this kind of resourcefulness.

Materials

Cleaned TV dinner tray, scissors, masking tape, scraps of colored paper, model-car or spray paint, string.

Procedure

- Place the tray upside down and measure it across to find the center. Make a mark and cut a slit at the top and bottom. (Figure A1)
- Cut out the largest indentation for the eye area. Immediately bind it with masking tape to prevent any

sharp edges. Overlap the cuts and bend the tray forward; curve it to fit the face. (Figure A2)

- Finally cut colored scrap paper to make a fringe and staple this strip to the top edge. Punch holes and tie string. The wearer is ready for a walk on the moon. (Figure B)
- If colored decorations are preferred, use model car paint or acrylics. Spray paint is also good if a solid color is the choice.

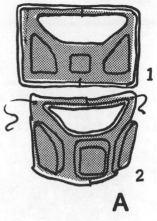

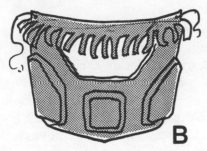

Lesson 10   Pariscraft Assembly Mask

Objectives

This lesson will enable children to become acquainted with a fairly new medium. Used in the medical field for making casts, it is ideal for masks and a variety of other art projects.

Materials

Newspaper for table, pariscraft, water, scissors, "Vaseline" Petroleum Jelly or cold cream.

Procedure

- Take a few minutes to refer back to the first part of the book for suggestions on working with pariscraft.
- This mask is a collection of features that can be interchanged to please the wearer. It is a matter of

creating your own expressions and combining them, such as eyes that are laughing with a mouth that is sad.

A

- Begin with the nose. Cut short strips of pariscraft; spread newspapers on the table; and have a bowl of water nearby. First cold cream the entire nose. Begin laying strips of pariscraft on the nose until no more than three layers are used. Let it dry for ten to twelve minutes, remove, trim edges, and let it dry. (Figure A)
- Make a narrow half mask and cover it with pariscraft, shaping it to curve the face. Gently lean it over the closed eyes to locate their position. (Figure B1) Cut eyes out and let them set to dry. (Figure B2)
- Apply cold cream around the mouth and design a mouth expression; build it up with layers of pariscraft and let it set as before. Remove and dry. (Figure C)
- Tie these on with a long, thin string or sewing elastic.

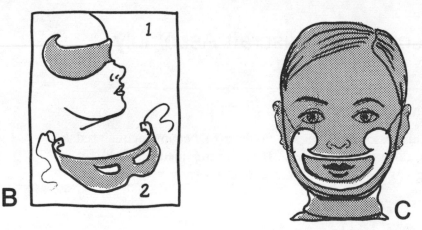

Bonus Ideas

Tie-Dye Head Mask

Use old sheeting. Cut the head mask to cover the whole head, or use an old pillow case. Plan the tie-dye pattern to relate to the features, or just tie-dye in any fashion and let dry. Remove string, press, and design the shape of the mask.

Paper Plate Mask

The lightweight, plain paper plates cost less and contain more in a package. Hold plate to face to determine eyes, nose, and mouth. Decorate first and then cut out eyes, end of nose, and mouth. Tie string to hold around the head.

Eyeglass and Nose Mask

Light-colored sunglasses are good if the pupil does not wear glasses. Draw a large funny nose and attach to bridge. Add long eyelashes to upper and lower rims. Attach with invisible tape, which is easy to remove.

Four Faces Grocery Mask

On each side of a grocery bag paint brightly colored faces. Make each different—smiling, crying, laughing, sleepy. Place bag on head and crush in the corners to fit the head.

Hound Dog Mask

Place grocery bag on head, using the narrow side for the face. Find area of eyes and mark, to be cut later. Cut bag from chin to ears. Make long, floppy ears at each side. Staple back of bag by overlapping to fit head.

Fingerpaint Mask

Two methods: First, use fingerpaint paper and make swirls in bright colors with the usual fingerpaint techniques. Then cut a full-face mask to fit. Second, draw the shape of the mask and its features with fingerpaint on dry paper. Then paint strokes to accent the features. Let dry and iron smooth.

Egg Box Mask

Use a long egg box, and remove the sections. Place it flat on the face and cut the shape you want. The slits are all ready for the eyes and make a different appearance. Paint in bright designs. Add strings for ties.

Horse's Head Mask

Two grocery bags are needed for this slightly older-group activity. The narrow end is the face of the horse, the bottom is the mouth and nostrils. Cut eyes, crush nostrils, and cut opening for mouth. Add ears. Now staple the second bag to this one, cutting out the base. Slit the four corners of the bag so it will slip over the shoulders. The base is used for the long, pointed ears.

Mosaic Mask

Cut a face mask, add brightly colored one-half inch squares, leaving paper spaces between mosaic pieces. Follow features.

Fabric Collage Mask and Wall Panel

Use fabric for skin, buttons for eyes, and so on. Let imagination soar to original fantasy ideas.

CHAPTER 6

"Show-off" Displays

*G*ay, bright, changing bulletin boards and display areas are important to a cheerful and modern classroom. Especially at the elementary level a need for new ideas is stimulating to both the child and the teacher. It is an added chore for the teacher, but creativity is part of learning experience for the pupils. In a larger room there could be a bulletin board on which the children plan, with supervision, their own ideas.

An area devoted to each month of the year is excellent; this can include current famous artists, artists of other fields, politicians, or famous sports figures.

To assist in keeping notices and displays eye-catching, bright in color and different in arrangement, here are some ideas that might prove inviting to the teacher.

Lesson 1   September "Get-Acquainted" Bulletin Board

Objectives

The opening of school in September offers many art ideas that can prove functional as well as being a good art lessons. Here each child has a chance to express himself by making a self-portrait to be used in a decorative way on bulletin boards and around the room.

Materials

Round paper plates, white drawing paper cut in squares (no larger than the recessed area of the plate), pencil, scissors, crayons, paste. A short pipe cleaner is optional for hanging the pictures.

Procedure

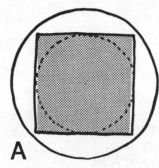

A

- To save paper and make it easier for the children to draw their heads the right size, cut white paper into squares in proportion to the recessed circle of the paper plate. (Figure A)
- Have them cut a circle by merely rounding off the corners.
- Most classrooms have a mirror, so if the children need to look in it for color of hair, eyes, or shape of nose, let them take a minute to do so. Have them color in their portrait and then retrim the head. Glue this self-portrait onto the recessed part of the paper plate and letter their first names on the rims. (Figure B)
- When all are finished, tack them up on the bulletin board for the class to view. Try many arrangements; three are shown in Figure C.

B

ANN

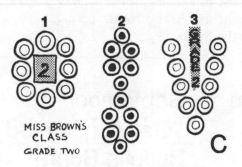

Lesson 2   Convertible Boxes for Display

Objectives

Children often create small items either as art forms or for social studies or science projects. Following is an attractive way to show them off on modern, brightly colored backgrounds.

Materials

Strong cartons, show boxes, strong cylinder containers, stationery boxes or durable candy boxes, spray paint, five bright poster colors, flat house paintbrush, water.

Procedure

- Always use odd numbers of objects to make any composition more interesting. This project calls for an odd number of variously shaped containers for the best effect.
- Paint the inside back panel of each container with a bright color and let dry. If the outside has commercial printing on it, spray paint the sides.
- Experiment with positioning of the containers. Two arrangements are shown in Figures A and B.
- If you have a setup that fits in a corner of the classroom and you feel it is appropriate, the boxes can be glued together. If not, keep them separate for different displays.

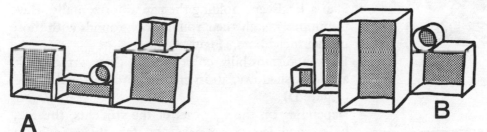

A   B

Lesson 3   Autumn Continuous
Room Border

Objectives

A continuous room border adds interest to the classroom and encourages the children to think in terms of cooperative work, at least in a simple way. From the border the children will observe autumn colors, noticing how sharp color patterns and blended hues complement each other, often within the same leaf.

Materials

White drawing paper (9″ x 12″), watercolor box or crayons, glue or stapler.

Procedure

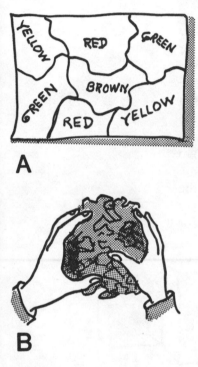

A

B

C

D

- Spread newspaper on the table. Open the watercolor box and wet the following colors: red, yellow, green, orange, and brown.
- Have extra small plastic cups ready. Pour three small puddles of water into the palette cover, keeping them separate, and two small puddles in the cups. Into these puddles add a color so the five colors are ready. Wet the paper with water and place splashes of these bright colors; try not to force them to run continuously into each other or a muddy brown tone will result. It should look like a patchwork quilt. (Figure A)
- While it is wet, pick up and crush in the hands into a ball, open it slightly and let it dry. (Figure B)
- Plan a landscape holding the paper horizontally. Have the pupils match their rolling foregrounds with those of their neighbors. (Figure C)
- Draw in distant hills, color the sky, draw a tree trunk, and cast shadows, all in crayons. Add a small house. (Figure D)
- Depending on the age level of the students, this may be a good lesson on near and far objects and the effect of distance on color. The sky is usually brighter overhead, near the top of the paper, and lighter near the hills. Let these remarks come from the children's discussion and observation.
- Take the dry, crushed colored paper, tear off about seven or nine small pieces, and fold up one end. Staple or glue the crushed foliage on top of the tree trunk. Glue these fallen leaves around on the ground under the tree, letting half of each piece bend up for a three-dimensional effect. (Figure E)
- Add a darker side to the tree to give a shadow effect to the trunk and lines for texture of the bark.
- The panels are ready to be tacked up side by side for a bright seasonal border.

Lesson 4   Decorative Classroom Mirrors

Objectives

Every classroom should have a mirror for many reasons: good grooming, identity study as in the life-size puppets, self-portraits, and as a place in the room for everyday and seasonal decorations.

Materials

A small 6″ x 9″ hanging mirror or an old wooden-framed mirror (many a home has an extra mirror to loan to the classroom), bits of left-over trimmings such as rickrack braid and ribbons, shell macaroni glued in a design and sprayed with gold paint, paper baking cups, Duco-cement, seasonal items.

Procedure

- Begin with a small mirror that has a narrow frame and fold baking cups in half. Count how many you will need and place them on the edge first for a formal arrangement. Then glue them in place with Duco-cement. (Figure A) In Figure A there are three examples: 1, the baking cups; 2, the shell macaroni; and 3, rickrack braid and centers of lace doilies.
- For small mirrors with too narrow a frame on which to glue designs, make separate cardboard frames for

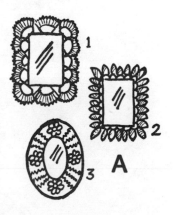

B

special days, as shown in Figure B: 1, Halloween paper sculpture owls; 2, Christmas; 3, birthdays; and 4, Easter eggs. Add originality to your classroom with decorative mirrors.

Lesson 5   Double Paper Plate Picture Mobile

Objectives

Children can make a mobile that creates an unusual display, especially in classrooms where bulletin board space is limited.

Materials

Paper plates (either oval or round), heavy cord, strong glue, scissors.

Procedure

- Place two plates upside down about one-eighth of an inch apart. Measure the heavy string or cord so it stretches across the two plates and allows for a loop at one end. (Figure A)
- Lift off the string and cover the base of the plate with Duco-cement or strong glue. Replace the string and immediately add a second plate on top of each lower plate. Place a heavy weight in the center to set and hold plates together. (Figure B)

A   **B**

- When set, it is ready to hang up. The plates will move around in the mobile principle, displaying both sides of the plates. (Figure C1) This would be a unique way to use the September self-portrait lesson discussed previously.
- See how easy it is to store this hanging display simply by stacking them together! (Figure C2)

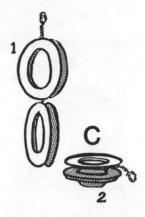

Lesson 6   Portable Towel Banner Display

Objectives

Sometimes a display is needed for a short duration, to be shown at the front of the room to illustrate a point. Here is an easy banner for children to make to which arithmetic papers or spelling papers can be attached, even by the children themselves. It can be hung anywhere in the room and later rolled up and stored away.

Materials

Old bath towel, beach size or regular; dowel post or straight branch, free of bark; brightly colored yarn; scissors; cardboard; a large needle for hand stitching (optional).

Procedure

- Clean the bark from the branch and paint it. Cut a notch at each end about one inch from the edges. Set it aside.
- Make the tassels. Cut a cardboard scrap the length you want the tassel to be. Wind yarn around it. (Figure A1) Slip a short piece of yarn under the looped yarn.
- Remove the cardboard and tie the looped yarn tightly. An inch down tie another piece of yarn around the loops and tie a knot. (Figure A2) Finally, cut the lower loops. (Figure A3)

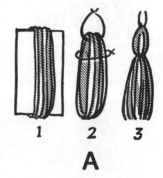

B

- Stitch the towel either by hand or machine. Slip the branch through the folded-over towel. Add the tassels and string to hang it up and the portable towel banner display is ready. (Figure B)

Lesson 7 Grow and Glow Christmas Tree

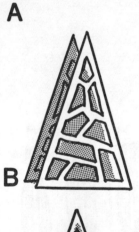

A

Objectives

Learning how to create an expanding design beginning with a 9" x 12" construction paper. Developing a design to be viewed from both sides.

Materials

Twenty-one sheets of 9" x 12" white, black, or colored construction paper, scissors, ruler, colored tissue paper, Duco-cement, pencil.

Procedure

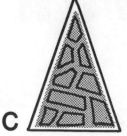

B

C

- Draw a diagonal line from the top right corner to the bottom left corner, holding the paper vertically. Measure up on the diagonal line 2-3/4", as illustrated in Figure A. Do the same to both triangles.
- Draw a half-inch line in from the edges on both papers. On one make abstract shapes with half-inch spaces between them. (Figure B)
- Cut out these areas. Then place the first pattern over the second triangle and draw shapes and cut them out also.
- Place one triangle on the table and cut a brightly colored tissue so that it covers into the half-inch frame. Glue it down. All the windows will have the same color. (Figure C)

- Glue the duplicate on top. This is one-tenth of the tree. Begin to build your tree, taping it to the window for it to grow and glow. (Figure D)
- Add a tub for the tree to stand in. Cut a double one and add red tissue.

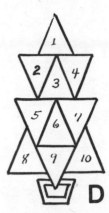

Lesson 8 Double Coat Hanger for Multiple Display

Objectives

Many times a small display is needed, especially in a room short of bulletin board space. The coat hanger can be used vertically or horizontally, serving as a basic structure for a mobile unit.

Materials

Two strong coat hangers, floral or masking tape.

Procedure

- Place two coat hangers on the table with the bases side by side. Tape them together. Form a little loop at the top if it is to be held vertically. (Figure A)
- This makes a basic structure for a mobile unit where the threads can be hung at various levels. (Figure B)
- Coat hangers and clip-on clothespins also create little displays. For added glamour, spray the hanger and a few clothespins with gold paint. Simply hang up the drawing, but fold a double piece of paper on the hanger first for a better grip with the clothespins. (Figure C)

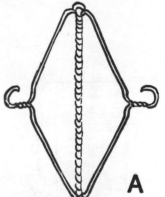

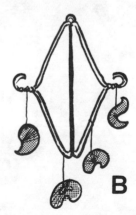

Lesson 9   The Versatile Rosette

Objectives

To learn simple, basic folding, both forward and backward, and to create rosettes that can be used singly or in multiple arrangements. Also, to explore a variety of papers for unusual effects.

Materials

Construction paper, wallpaper, colored tissue, scissors, glue, stapler, stringbands are helpful for holding in place.

Procedure

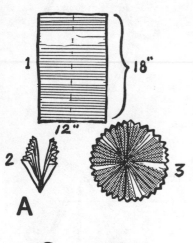

- Begin with any lightweight scrap paper and fold without measuring for practice first; ordinary 6" x 9" math paper is a good size to use, however, it will be necessary to glue two sheets together to make it long enough to fold and spread into a circle.
- After practicing, measure a 12" x 18" piece of lightweight paper (poster paper is good) into half-inch bands. (Figure A1) Fold forward on the first line and backwards on the second, until all are folded; then fold in half. (Figure A2)
- Join the two ends to make a rosette. (Figure A3)
- Various arrangements can be made. (Figure B) Window Christmas tree, hanging P.T.A. decorations, and a window box of spring flowers made from colorful wallpaper are some suggestions.
- Further ideas can be used, including tiered hanging rosettes, hanging birds with two rosette wings, and a box with two pencils for supports for the four wheel rosettes. (Figure C)

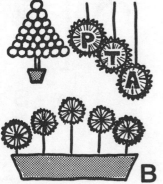

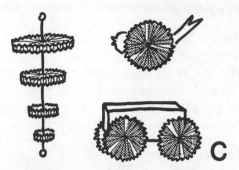

Lesson 10   Egg Box Christmas Display

Objectives

The ordinary egg box is ideal for any kind of Christmas display. However, it is especially good for the theme of the twelve days before Christmas. If the twelve symbols in the song are too difficult for your grade level to make, let them use Christmas ideas of their own.

Materials

Egg box, ribbon rosette, spray paint or poster paint to color the interior of the shelves, tinsel, old Christmas cards, plasticine or Play-Doh to make symbols, glue.

Procedure

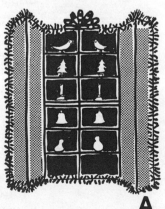

- First paint the inside of the shelf background with bright red or a color of your choice.
- Trim the outside edge with tinsel, either by stapling it in place or gluing it.
- Now cut partridges, pears, Christmas trees, candles, stars, and other ornaments out of old Christmas cards and glue to the shelves, or make them out of plasticine or Play-Doh and glue to the shelf. This makes a stand-alone display. (Figure A)

Bonus Ideas

Crepe Paper Harvest Display

Crepe paper must be handled with dry hands. Use the length of the sheet for a large pumpkin. Experiment with width needed. Tie ends together and turn inside out. Stuff with crushed newspaper. Twist the top closed and tie; wind green crepe paper around to form thick stem. Flatten pumpkin slightly to rest on table. Make other fruits and vegetables for a table harvest display.

Touch and Feel Texture Display

This display is an excellent way to stimulate ideas for story illustrations. Cut freeform shapes and staple to a special easy-to-reach bulletin board. Use sandpaper, leather, fur, metal, and tree bark (oak, birch, etc.).

Old Classroom Map Display

Instead of throwing out an outdated pull-down map, use it for a display. Cover it with sheeting or burlap or paint it using spray paint or calcimine. Children can hang up their own spelling papers or art work. A pull-down, painted shade or map can also be used for a mural. When finished, repaint and it is ready for a new theme.

Paper Baking Cup Snapshot Display

Mark off a section on the bulletin board for a children's snapshot display. Since the photos are small, simply flatten pastel-colored paper baking cups and tack to wall. With masking tape rolled sticky side out, adhere to the snapshot; it is easily removed for another display.

Record Player Merry-Go-Round

At the nongrooved center area of a record, adhere little figures with masking tape. Back them so they will stand firmly. Glue fringes of colored tissue paper on top of heads. Play the record and watch the figures swing around on the record to music with fringe flying in the air.

String Room Divider

To hide an untidy corner or work area, use lengths of string strung with different colored beads and secure to ceiling or beam. Strips of fireproof crepe paper will also make an attractive divider for a particular occasion.

Classroom Decorated Wastebaskets

Use large grocery bags. Spray paint with soft colors to match decor of the classroom. Let children decorate with markers or glue a favorite picture on the front. Insert a stone in the bottom of the bag to keep it in a standing position.

Hanging Box Picture Display

Select a 7" or 9" box. Cut pictures depicting a theme, season, sport, or story read in class. Glue pictures on the six sides. Open cover and tie string exactly in center through picture; glue cover shut. Hung from the ceiling, you have a revolving display.

Real Branches with Art-Lesson Leaves

On white drawing paper draw freehand autumn leaves. Discuss the beautiful color combinations. Brush clear water over the drawing and splash bright colors (no black or blue). Let colors blend into each other. Let dry, attach to branches, and display.

Giant, Crepe Paper Wall Displays

These can be used for plays as well. Make huge blossoms of daisies, tulips, and other flowers. Also good for panels where a seasonal theme is needed for P.T.A. night or other function.

CHAPTER 7

Flower Explosion

Materials of all colors, textures, and designs are readily available for making flowers. Real or imaginary flowers can be created from a variety of materials ranging from the simple plastic bag to exotic fabric, and from dried foods to scraps of paper.

Motivation can come from field trips, far-away cultures, slides, color reproductions, and many other sources. Seasonal plants and blossoms can result in enthusiastic art lessons. Learning the skill of creatively using household items for flowers can become a challenge to the pupil and result in unusual classroom displays.

Try experimenting with a variety of inexpensive materials and have a good deal of fun!

Lesson 1   Plastic Bag Flowers

Objectives

Experimenting with small, transparent, plastic bags to make imaginary flowers.

Materials

Small plastic bags, green pipe cleaners, white paper cup, earth to fill cup, quick-drying spray paint (optional).

Procedure

- Open the plastic bag and blow a small amount of air into it.
- Gather the open end, and, before twisting a pipe cleaner to close it, test to be sure the bag is a little soft. Then continue to twist the pipe cleaner tightly. (Figure A)

- Pull the pipe cleaner over the top of the bag to divide it into two oval buds; secure leaving a stem. (Figure B)

A B

C

- Fold up the left-over part of the bag to form a shell around the two buds. (Figure C) Plant the flower in the cup.
- If a light color is desired, set the flower in a lump of plasticine and spray in a spray booth.

Lesson 2   Magazine Page Chrysanthemum

Objectives

Experimenting with folding and cutting to make imaginative flowers.

Materials

Brilliantly colored magazine pages, scissors, yarn, pipe cleaners, container with earth to plant the blossom.

Procedure

- Fold the magazine page in half and fold again. (Figure A)
- Fold the top half down and draw three petals. (Figure B)
- Cut the folded paper petals, then open the page to

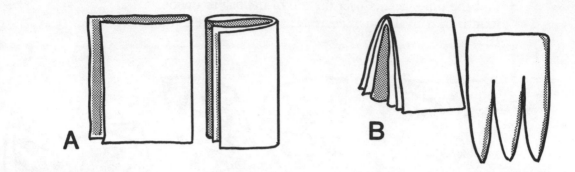

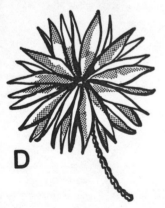

find twelve petals on the top edge and twelve on the bottom, a total of twenty-four in all. (Figure C1)

- Gather the center together and tie with yarn. (Figure C2) Yarn is better than string to work with because it doesn't cut the paper as quickly. Twist a pipe cleaner around the center. Press the center of the chrysanthemum and fan out the petals. (Figure D) The brilliant colors of the magazine page make a colorful flower. A small container can be filled with earth and the flower planted, or use the flower as a bulletin-board display by stapling them in a design.

Lesson 3   Perky Fabric Flowers

Objectives

To make use of colorful fabric remnants to create imaginary flowers.

Materials

Scraps of gaily colored fabrics, odd buttons, pipe cleaners, easy-to-cut cardboard, glue and vase (if desired), scissors, waxed paper.

Procedure

- Decide on the size and number of petals for the flower. Cut a circle the size of the flower out of the cardboard. Cover the circle with strong glue and place the petals on it gathering them a little at the base; cover with a piece of waxed paper and press. (Figure A)

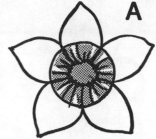

- Remove the waxed paper and add a little more glue to the center; select a button that contrasts with the fabric and adhere to the center. (Figure B) Let it set.
- Turn the flower over and glue a pipe cleaner on the back. (Figure C)
- The result is a perky flower to complement a bulletin board, vase, or flower box.
- The single flower can also be used for a drawing lesson. Ask the children to use their imaginations and color a setting for their blossom, then staple or glue the flower in place.

Lesson 4 Cotton Ball Centerpiece and Placecard

Objectives

To use household items for creative art ideas.

Materials

Cotton balls, scraps of green construction paper, scissors, pipe cleaners, paper drinking cup, ribbon (optional), marker, glue, colored chalk.

Procedure

- Twist pipe cleaners together to make a strong stem. Add glue at the end and push it inside a cotton ball.

A

Let it set. Do this to three or five balls. Odd numbers make a better design. Rub chalk on paper and dust the cotton balls in it.

- Cut long, slender leaves from the green construction paper and curl them over a pencil. Puncture the base of the cup and twist the bouquet into it.
- Add a ribbon for extra color and, if used for a placecard, letter the name of the guest at the lower rim. (Figure A)

Lesson 5   Crushed Rose Colonial Bouquet

Objectives

To learn how to handle crepe paper to form roses, creating gifts of corsages and bouquets for parties and other events.

Materials

Crepe paper, scissors, 5" paper doilies, green crepe-paper streamers, green construction paper, pencil, pipe cleaners, paste, stapler.

Procedure

- Cut a 5" x 7" strip of crepe paper on the grain.
- Place it on the table and rest a pencil on the 5" width.
- Roll the crepe paper around the pencil lightly. (Figure A)
- Hold the ends of the crepe paper with both hands and push the crepe paper together. (Figure B)

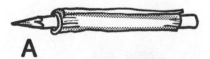

A

B

- Gently unwind it almost to the end. (Figure C1)
- Holding the curved part at the base, wrap it around until it forms a bud. (Figure C2) Twist a pipe cleaner around it.
- Cut a small, green construction-paper circle and glue it to the back center of the lace doily. Cut into the center from the edge and cut a few radial slits at the center.
- Cut three or four slivers of green construction paper and wrap around the bud. Then insert into the opening. Overlap the cut doily to a concave form and staple in place.
- Finally wrap the stem with a short, green crepe-paper streamer. The colonial bouquet or corsage is ready for a gift. (Figure D)

Lesson 6   Kaleidoscope Flowers

Objectives

This lesson provides an opportunity to experiment with color and shapes for creative flower making.

Materials

Two **9″ x 12″** sheets of colored tissue paper (same color), newspaper, scissors, thin wire, waterproof glue (such as Duco-cement), waxed paper, flat brush, a solution of one-half water and one-half Elmer's Glue-All.

Procedure

- Cover your work table with newspaper. Tear off a sheet of waxed paper larger than the colored tissue. Place this on the newspaper and add one sheet of colored tissue.
- Cut and tear small bits of tissue and set aside for later use.
- With the flat brush spread the glue and water solution over the tissue paper. Place the colored scrap shapes in whatever design you wish. When it is ready, place

A

the second sheet of colored tissue over this colorful pattern.

- Place another sheet of waxed paper over this to make a smooth, flat surface.
- Immediately remove both sheets of waxed paper and place on a fresh sheet to dry.
- It will be stiff when dry. At that time cut out freeform flowers and lay them flat on the table. Curl the ends of the wire and glue in place. (Figure A)
- Small and large flowers can be made in this way. Placed in a window they will look like a kaleidoscope!

Lesson 7   No-paste Flower Collage

Objectives

This is a pleasant dry lesson with no pasting involved. It employs a functional item that can be used as a colorful art lesson.

Materials

Self-adhesive paper in wood grain, marble, brick, floral, plain, and other patterns, scissors, pencil, cardboard backing.

Procedure

A

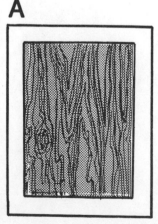

- Plan the entire collage panel including what backing is to be used, the size of the flowers, what patterns to use, and so on.
- The opportunities are endless, but for this example the wood-grained pattern will be used for a background. Select a piece of white cardboard, decide on the width of a border and cut the wood-grained paper to fit the space allowed. Peel off the backing and adhere to the cardboard. (Figure A)
- Select color combinations and patterns. Turn the self-adhesive paper on the wrong side and draw a variety of flowers, stems, and leaves. Do not remove

the backing until you have experimented with different compositions.

- Then peel off the backing and arrange the flower collage. (Figure B)
- This lesson will result in a variety of individual designs. A further functional use for such flower collages is to decorate paper bags, making gift tote bags.

B

Lesson 8   Pastel Baking Cup Blossoms

Objectives

If you are searching for inexpensive materials to use for classroom flower construction, the paper baking cup package, which contains eighty-eight cups, will supply enough material for twenty-two flowers.

Materials

One package of pastel baking cups, pipe cleaners, scissors, green crepe-paper streamers, stapler. Container is optional.

A

Procedure

- Fold a pink paper cup in half and roll into a spiral.
- Fold a second pink cup and roll around the first for a full center of the flower. (Figure A) Staple the base.
- Select a blue cup and cut in the center base. Take a second blue cup and flatten it.
- Insert the pink double center through the two cups and secure with a pipe cleaner. Staple in place since a pipe cleaner can slip off the baking cup.
- Staple a green crepe-paper streamer to the base and begin to twist it around the stem, pulling in a diagonal manner so it will fit tightly around the pipe cleaner.
- Add leaves if they suit the decoration.
- Stand it in a small container for a lovely display. (Figure B)

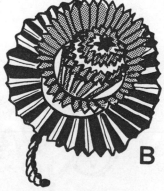

B

Lesson 9 Wallpaper Spiral Flowers

Objectives

This lesson involves practically no expense, especially when wallpaper companies are willing to give away old wallpaper books. These are filled with large and small, bright and dull designs, giving full creative range to flower makers!

Materials

Old wallpaper book, scissors, wallpaper paste, pipe cleaners, green crepe-paper streamers, stapler.

Procedure

- There are only two parts to this bouncing spiral flower. For the center cut two 3″ x 4″ strips of colorful wallpaper. Paste them together and let them dry flat.
- Cut a fringe on the 4″ length, keeping within 1″ of the base. Place a pencil on the 3″ width and roll around the pencil, open, and roll so curled fringe turns inward. (Figure A)

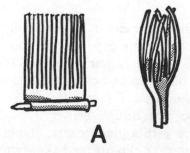

A

B

- Follow the same procedure with the two 3″ x 10″ strips. This time, however, when the fringe has been curled, roll so the fringe bends outward.
- Wrap the large one around the small center and secure with a pipe cleaner. (Figure B)
- Tightly twist the green crepe-paper streamer around the stem and staple it in place.

- Practice with different colors and patterns pasted together.

Lesson 10 Egg Noodle Bow Sprays

Objectives

Colorful sprays are easy to make and ideal for any seasonal bulletin-board display. They are also a good decoration for P.T.A. night. Using ready-made, inexpensive, egg-noodle bows results in easy lessons with colorful results.

Materials

Box of egg-noodle bows, pipe cleaners, bright, quick-drying spray paint.

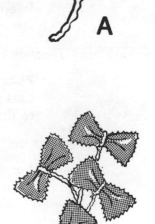

A

Procedure

- Twist a pipe cleaner around the center indentation of the bow. The noodle is strong enough to take quite a bit of handling. (Figure A)
- Twist a second bow and add it to the stem of the first, continuing in this way until a spray of bows is made.
- For the final step, spread newspaper on the table and, placing the egg noodle arrangement in the center, spray with a bright, quick-drying enamel paint. This not only adds a shiny coating, but strengthens the entire spray. (Figure B)
- Egg-noodle shells can be used as single buds and make an unusual and attractive display if you spray paint with a variety of colors.

B

Bonus Ideas

Waxed Paper and Button Flowers

Open a waxed paper or plastic sandwich bag. In the center of the base wire a button (use a pipe cleaner if you have no wire). Then gather the open end and twist into a stem.

Stitchery Flower Panel

Use a long vertical piece of window screening, and stitch imaginary flowers in bright colors. Mount on heavy paper for contrast.

Lace Doily Flowers

Use small lace doilies in white, silver, or gold. Simply pinch the center and cup the doily by pulling through the semiclosed hand. Twist the stem to make a large or small bud.

Cellophane Drinking Straw Carnations

Cut drinking straws in half. Lay them on the table and place a wire or pipe cleaner in the center. Tie the wire or twist it making the straws form a sunburst. Add a long stem—either a pipe cleaner or another single straw.

Yarn and Button Flowers

Wind yarn around a 3″ piece of cardboard. Use multicolored left-over yarns or just use one color. Slip off and tie in the center. Attach a brightly colored button using the ends of the yarn.

Toothpick and Pipe Cleaner Flowers

Place waxed paper on table. Glue toothpicks into sunburst designs. Curl the end of a colored pipe cleaner in a small spiral shape and glue to the center of the toothpick flower. Let dry.

Beads on Wire Flowers

For your art projects you can purchase beads or simply use those from a broken strand. Wire them according to your color tastes and loop them into petals. Secure a stem, making a dainty corsage.

Pariscraft Water Lily

Cut a disk about 4″ in diameter for the base. Keep hands dry while cutting many long, pointed petals. Dip a 4″ piece of pariscraft in warm water and gently crush. Place on the center of the cardboard disk. Dip each petal in water and secure at the base of the center, curling it over the center shape. Continue until the cardboard base is filled. If a petal seems to fall down, simply support it with a small ball of crushed newspaper until dry. For a more lifelike water lily, make double petals.

Melted Crayon Flat Flowers

Draw an outline of a blossom on paper. Light a short candle in a tin can. Place the crayon in the flame for a second and immediately apply to the drawing. Continue until the flower has the right color combinations. Shellac when dry to prevent breaking if handled too often. This is called *encaustic*.

Paper Sculpture Flowers

Decide on the flower shape, then cut petal and roll over a round pencil; make a center with small crushed white paper and surround this with the sculptured petals. Do the same with the leaves, keeping the stem flat.

CHAPTER 8

Happy Hats

*T*hroughout the centuries hats have been worn for various reasons. They were worn for protection against climate, for fashionable adornment, and for recognition of rank and religious affiliations.

Hat making can become an interesting art project when hats are needed for a play or seasonal activity. The study of history and cultures will reveal hats of every description. These observations can lead to a variety of hat creations where color, design, and imagination are combined through the talents of the little artist.

Children love to dress up in these hats for fashion parades, in plays, and at parties for the holidays.

Lesson 1 Witches' Hat and Hair

Objectives

Seasonal activities are important in all grades and Halloween is especially fun for young children. It is even more fun to make your own costume, especially the hat.

Materials

Paper plate, paper drinking cup, glue, scissors, yarn, string or ribbon, quick-drying spray paint.

Procedure

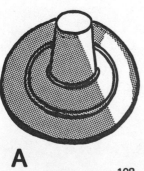

- Turn the paper plate upside down and glue the drinking cup, also inverted, in the center. (Figure A) Place a heavy book on the cup to hold it until the glue sets.

A

- If the hat is to be sprayed black or orange, do it now.
- To decide on the hair, place the hat on the head and mark off the width of the bangs and their length. Cut yarn in short strips. Decide on the length of the side and back hair and cut strips of yarn. The yarn hair can be glued or taped. When the glue is set, turn the hat upright and attach ribbons. It is ready for the small witch. (Figure B)

B

Lesson 2   Tissue Pleated Hat

Objectives

To make a hat out of a minimum of materials. This is an easy-to-make hat with no paste or scissors used.

Materials

Colored tissue paper, masking tape, tape measure, two rulers, invisible tape.

Procedure

- Place two sheets of colored tissue paper side by side and tape with invisible tape. This makes a 36″ strip.
- Measure around the head of the wearer, allowing two extra inches.
- Lightly tack the tape on the table and divide in half, marking with a pencil.
- Lay the tissue one inch in from the edge of the tape and do this below the tape. Pleat the tissue up to the halfway mark and place a ruler over the pleats to hold. Crease them so sharp pleats are seen. Hold this down with two rulers. (Figure A)

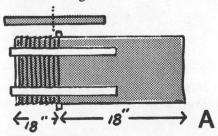

A

- Complete pleating the other half, again using the ruler.
- Lift the tape and press firmly onto the pleats, two-thirds of the way down; the deeper part of the pleats will form the crown. (Figure B) Overlap the tape ends and close the top.
- The pleated hat is ready for the wearer to model. (Figure C)

B

C

Lesson 3   Giant Newspaper Hat

Objectives

Newspaper is an ideal material to use in making hats, especially when experimenting. Since most classrooms have a generous supply of newspapers, there need be no concern about wasting materials.

Materials

Plenty of newspaper, scissors, stapler, ruler, pencil, spray paint. Ribbons or string are optional.

Procedure

- Spread two double pages together on the table.
- Measure in 6½" on the short end and cut off. (Figure A)
- Wrap this double strip around the head for size and staple in place. (Figure B1) Cut slits on the top edge, overlap, and staple. (Figure B2)

A

B

- The remainder of the newspaper forms a square. With a large blackboard compass draw a circle to touch the edges. Draw a smaller circle to fit the head about 7″ in diameter. (Figure C)
- Cut slits on the inner circle from the center to the 7″ diameter. Fold these triangles up. Put paste on the outside and slip the crown over these, pressing into place. Let it set.
- A giant newspaper hat results. Staple or paste the edges of the large rim in a few places. Add a ribbon and the hat is ready for fun and fashion. (Figure D)

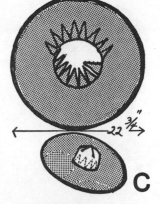

Lesson 4   TV Dinner Tray Hat

Objectives

To learn how to utilize TV dinner trays. Usually they are used to mix paint in, but try experimenting with hat making. They have good possibilities, and here is one to try.

Materials

Thoroughly washed and dried TV dinner tray, two pastel paper baking cups, a length of bulky bright-colored yarn, scissors, stapler.

Procedure

- Cut a slit on each long side, in the center, and staple by overlapping to fit the head. (Figure A)

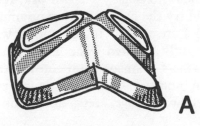

B

- Punch holes on the short sides, nearer the back, and insert bulky yarn and tie in place.
- Fold a paper cup in half and roll in spiral shape; fold back the base and glue in the center of a second cup. Use waterproof glue. Then glue the flower on the side of the hat. Let it set. The result is a perky, shiny, expensive-looking hat. (Figure B)

Lesson 5   Pariscraft Basic Hat

Objectives

To become acquainted with the medium of pariscraft and at the same time make a basic hat form to be decorated with ideas of the pupils. All sorts of themes can be used.

Materials

Pariscraft, scissors, newspapers, water, bowl, bathing cap, additional materials for decorating, acrylics or spray paint (optional).

A

Procedure

- There are many ways to shape the pariscraft and let it dry to form a basic hat. A bathing cap can be worn and strips of pariscraft dipped in water and crisscross layered on top. Or, the cap can be stuffed with crushed newspapers and placed in a bowl, which will prevent it from rolling around. (Figure A)
- When the bathing cap is ready, cut strips of pariscraft about 6" long and dip in warm water; smooth out over the cap until three layers are formed. Bind the edges for more comfortable handling.
- When thoroughly set and dry, remove the newspaper and try the hat on. Dream up unusual themes. (Figure B) Here are an insect and a warrior—both can be brightly colored. The nose guard, chin strap, and feathers are made from construction paper.
- An unusual hat for a dance could be made with yellow, orange, red, and pink tissue-paper petals

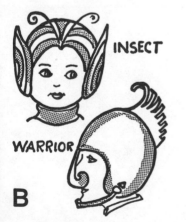

INSECT

WARRIOR

B

simply glued at the base with waterproof glue. (Figure C) The remaining petals stand up in a blaze of colors.

Lesson 6 Brown Paper Bag Hat

Objectives

With brown paper bags easily available, each child can make a hat for himself. Colorful additions can be made from scraps of colored construction and tissue paper.

Materials

Brown paper bag, scissors, scraps of colored paper, glue, stapler, short piece of masking tape (optional).

Procedure

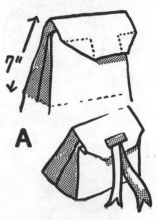

- Select a bag with a square bottom, not the envelope style.
- Open the bag just enough to leave the square base slightly folded over. Fold the corners under; glue or tape this flap to the back of the bag. Measure down 7″ and cut off. (Figure A)
- Cut two streamers from the base and tape or glue on the back flap.
- Shape the front of the hat (the whole edge could be scalloped), however, the simple curve is effective. (Figure B)
- Use scraps of colored paper to make flowers, feathers, and other decorations. This is a durable hat to be worn either sideways or front side forward, with or without the flowers.

Lesson 7 Comedian's Hat

Objectives

To learn to use other ideas with paper plates, which come in all shapes and colors.

Materials

Paper plates, scissors, scraps of colored paper, glue, ruler, pencil, pipe cleaners.

Procedure

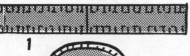

- Select a flat-rimmed plate, and cut into the flat rim from the edge. Cut out the inside circle and save. (Figure A)
- Cut two strips of paper 12" x 3" and tape or glue them to form one long piece. Measure down from the top and bottom ½" and draw a line on top and bottom edge. Cut slits in from the edges all along both sides. (Figure B1) Fold these forward. Run glue on the bottom tabs and also on the rim. Press this strip in place and join the ends.
- Let it set. Then place glue on the top (bent tabs forward) and set the center of the plate on them. (Figure B2) Let it set. This completes the crown of the hat. Add a pipe cleaner with a gay flower at the end. Decorate the hat band, or spray the whole hat before decorating.
- The hat is ready for the comedian's performance. (Figure C)

Lesson 8   Circle Hat

Objectives

There is no waste in making this hat since the basic part is cut from one sheet of 9" x 12" construction paper. The child can fit the hat to his or her head. This hat can either be used in the first stage and decorated, or a crepe-paper circle can be added.

Materials

Sheet of construction paper, scissors, crepe paper, paste, sequins or scraps of colored paper for decorations.

Procedure

- Draw a circle the full size of the paper (9″ diameter).
- Draw a smaller circle in the center using a diameter of 5¾″.
- Draw radiation lines from the center using a ruler, or cut freehand. (Figure A) Fold out. The hat can be left at this stage and the points decorated with sequins or flowers. (Figure B)
- If a completed hat with a crown is needed, simply cut a circle from crepe paper measuring 7½″ in diameter.
- Brush paste on all the points keeping it flat on the table. Waxed paper underneath is helpful in cleanup. Place the circle on the head, immediately place the crepe paper on top, hold, and shape in place until it sticks enough.
- The final touch is to make your own flowers and glue around the rim to cover the edge of the shallow crown. (Figure C)

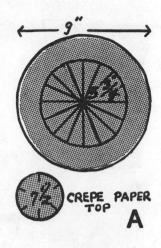

CREPE PAPER TOP **A**

B

C

Lesson 9 Pillowcase Mouse Hood

Objectives

Here is a hat for fun and games that the teacher can easily store away for those rainy days. An old pillowcase is ideal for this unusual hat.

Materials

Old pillowcase, string, scissors, newspapers, colored markers (optional).

Procedure

- Crush a double sheet of newspaper into a corner of the pillowcase and tie with a string. (Figure A) Do the same to the other corner.
- Slip the pillowcase over the head and draw the facial features with a pencil. Make curved lines over the eyebrows and cut that section out. Slit the back. (Figure B)
- Slip the bag over the head and tie under the chin. The mouse hood is ready for parties, Halloween night, or for play acting. (Figure C)

A

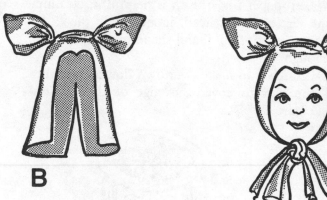

B

C

Lesson 10   Jester's Hat with Bell

Objectives

To teach the children to experiment with original designs for hats. To make hats with fewer tools and more ideas.

Materials

Newspapers, scissors, tape or stapler, spray paint (optional).

Procedure

- Place the folded double sheet of newspaper around the head with the fold at the forehead. Determine how tight it should be and staple the ends.

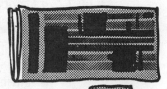

- Fold the cylinder shape flat and draw the shape of a jester's hat in pencil. (Figure A)
- Cut on this line and staple or tape the edges. Tie a small bell at the end of the hat.
- Either leave the hat as newsprint, paint brightly colored designs on it, or spray paint it a solid color.
- It is already being enjoyed by the wearer! (Figure B)

Bonus Ideas

Paper-Sculpture Bird Hat

Measure from ear over head to ear, this is the diameter of a circle needed for hat. Cut four slits—front, back, and sides about 4" deep toward center. Overlap and staple. Cut two patterns of head and beak; glue together except where head is joined to hat; spread open and adhere. Make three wing patterns, large, medium, and small; glue large ones first to sides of hat, then remaining others on top.

Indian Squaw Headdress

Grocery bags are ideal for this since both white and colored crayons show up well on this surface. Cut a wide band and decorate with Indian designs; add a single brightly colored feather in back.

Robin Hood Hat

Fold rectangular paper in half and mark the center on folded edge. Bend the folded edge to make a right angle—do this to both sides, leaving a strip to be bent over each side. Open the hat and bend the back up. Add a feather. This is the fold-a-paper-cup, newspaper boat, or soldier's hat idea.

Clown Pompom Hat

Newspaper is the least expensive for this since the project requires a lot of paper. Roll a double sheet of newspaper into a cone shape, staple. Tie ribbons at each side and tie under chin. Spray paint a bright color and add a yarn pompom at the top.

Crepe-Paper Pumpkin Hat

Follow directions for making a crepe-paper harvest pumpkin in chapter 6. A stem is the top of the hat.

Valentine Hat

Measure from the front of the head to the center of the back—this is the widest part of the heart. Draw two large red hearts that will fit the head when stapled together. Use a drinking straw for the stem and add small hearts resembling leaves.

Pirate Hat

Use old sheeting or an old colorful scarf. Tie on head with knot at left ear. Staple a black patch on the scarf to cover one eye.

Windmill Hat

Make the crown as directed for a paper-sculpture bird hat, the first bonus idea in this chapter. Make five small windmills, each a different color as in lesson 1 of chapter 10.

Pipe Cleaner Hat with Flowers

Make a ring by twisting pipe cleaners to fit the head. Cut flat paper flowers and staple to a pipe cleaner every two inches. Make four of these and join to ring—front, back and two sides. Add more flowers to the ring for a gay little hat.

Papier-Mâché Hat with Fantasy Ideas

Find a mixing bowl, preferably plastic, that fits the head. Cover with strips of paper dipped in wallpaper paste. Cover with three layers for durability. Decide on the fantasy idea and add appropriate features. Spray the hat white and decorate imaginatively.

CHAPTER 9

Priceless Picture Frames

*Y*our young artists will be well motivated if they know they will have an opportunity to display their work. Therefore, plan to set aside some time for the children to design and make frames that will complement what they have made. Let them decide how to arrange their work, and they will have their own art gallery.

A variety of materials, inexpensive and easy to handle, can be developed into interesting and effective frames. Styles of all kinds can be designed, including mobile hanging frames, stand-up ones, refillable ones, and many others discussed in this chapter. Let children experiment in harmonious settings for their art and you will find that priceless picture frames result.

Lesson 1   Pariscraft Slide-in Picture Frame

Objectives

Pariscraft is a popular medium in art classes. Many ideas originate from this material, which is enjoyed by the children. A novel idea is to use it in frame making. Pariscraft frames are easy to construct and durable.

Materials

Pariscraft, bowl of water, scissors, ruler, pencil, pad of newspapers, waxed paper.

Procedure

- Set up the work area with plenty of newspapers and other materials.

- Tear off a sheet of 9" x 12" waxed paper. This is a good size to start with. Have plenty of newspapers extending past the waxed paper. (Figure A)
- Cut enough strips of pariscraft to cover the waxed paper three times. Set these aside, away from the water. (When drops of water fall on the pariscraft it becomes hard and is not reusable.)
- Dip the first strip in water, press together slightly, and smooth it out on the waxed paper beginning at the top edge. Press with your hands flat until wrinkles are gone. Repeat this step until the waxed paper has been covered three times.
- When dry enough to mark with a pencil, draw a 6" x 9" rectangle on the pariscraft, this is the size of drawing for this frame. It is a good size to practice with.
- Cut a strip of pariscraft 9" long and dip in water and fold twice.
- Press one half of this strip onto the background so the fold is on the line. Repeat for the bottom line. (Figure B) Be sure the top half is slightly open to allow the drawing to be slipped inside the runners.
- To finish the edges of the frame and to make it look more realistic, cut some strips the length of the four sides. Dip each in water, press slightly, and smooth onto the sides of the frame. Cut diagonally at the corners for a mitered look. Add a loop for hanging the frame, but be sure it is centered so the picture will hang straight. (Figure C)

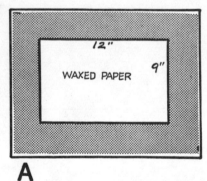

A

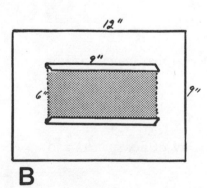

B

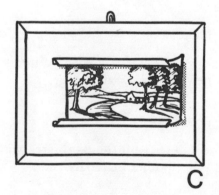

C

Lesson 2 Corrugated Cardboard Frame

Objectives

To learn to utilize discarded pencil-box covers and create frames with three-dimensional material.

Materials

Empty corrugated pencil-box covers, white or colored corrugated cardboard, black construction paper, scissors, stapler, glue, scraps of white paper.

Procedure

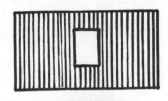

- If empty corrugated box covers are available, simply turn them inside out to reveal a white inside. These box covers come with a handsome oval cutout, ideal for a miniature flower display. (Figure A)

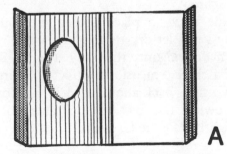

A

B

- Cut a piece of black construction paper to fit inside of the box and cut tiny flowers, pasting them on this paper within the oval dimensions. Paste in place in box cover.
- If pencil boxes are not available, simply cut a piece of corrugated cardboard the height and width you want. Cut a rectangular or oval opening. Measure a sheet of black or colored paper so it will appear in the window. (Figure B)
- Plan paper sculpture so it will show to advantage on the backdrop when it is stapled in cylinder form. (Figure C)

C

Lesson 3 Craft Stick Refillable Frame

Objectives

To learn how to make a picture frame with craft sticks that is easily refillable.

Materials

Craft sticks, glue, 12" x 18" and 9" x 12" construction paper.

Procedure

- On the 12" x 18" construction paper place a smaller piece of 9" x 12" paper and draw around it.
- Do not glue immediately, just arrange the craft sticks in place. The top row will extend beyond the 9" x 12" paper just enough to form a pleasant design. (Figure A)
- Glue these in place adding the four corner sticks. Press and let dry thoroughly. When ready, slip a 9" x 12" drawing into the frame. (Figure B)
- If a three-dimensional effect is desired, just fold the two sides back about an inch. Glue or staple in place, allowing the picture in frame to curve outward slightly. (Figure C)
- For a revolving frame with double pictures, glue two 12" x 18" finished frames together and suspend by a thin string.

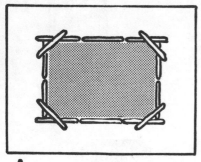

A

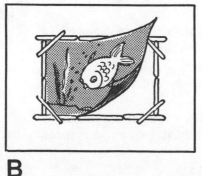

B

C

Lesson 4   Toothpick Frame

Objectives

Children enjoy working with toothpicks and this is a good way to introduce handling them and at the same time create a frame that is unique and attractive.

Materials

Flat toothpicks, 12" x 18" construction paper, scissors. (A box of toothpicks contains 750, and makes seven frames. Each frame contains about 100 toothpicks.)

Procedure

- Hold the construction paper horizontally and measure 15" across. Cut off the three inches and save for other projects.
- Draw the 9" x 12" inner border, and mark off the eight places as illustrated in Figure A.
- Run a line of waterproof glue on these eight lines and adhere the eight toothpicks. Press and let them set.
- It is easier to begin at the corners slanting the toothpicks at first and straightening them at the center points. Do this on all four sides. (Figure B)
- To display a drawing, merely roll masking tape with its sticky side out and attach to each corner. Then press onto the toothpick frame. Add a loop to hang it up for all to admire.

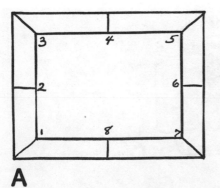

A

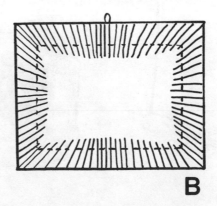

B

Lesson 5 Square-base Paper Bag Frame

Objectives

We all welcome lessons involving inexpensive materials such as this one. The paper bag frame is easy to make and attractive, too.

Materials

Square-base paper bag, scissors, pencil. String, yarn, or spray paint are optional.

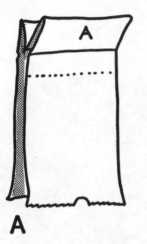

A

Procedure

- Fold up the flap "A" and measure down 2", or the depth you would like the frame to be. (Figure A) Draw a line across on both sides.
- Open the bag and cut from each corner to the line. (Figure B)
- With a long pencil roll up each side as far as the paper bag is cut and slide the pencil out. (Figure C)
- Cut a sheet of construction paper the size of the base of the bag and either draw a picture or mount paper sculpture on it. Push it into the frame; if it is cut exactly the same size, its tight fit will hold it in place.
- There are two ways to hang it up. One is simply to thumbtack it to the bulletin board. The other is to run a brightly colored string through the three curled rolls and hang it up as illustrated in Figure D.

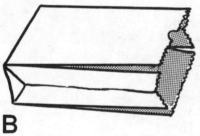

B

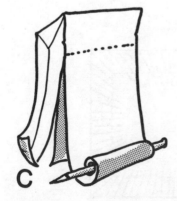

C

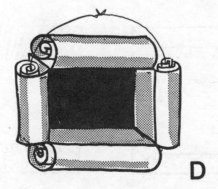

D

Lesson 6   Stand-up Box Cover Frame

Objectives

By saving discarded box covers, interesting frames can be made. These are especially attractive for P.T.A. night art work display.

Materials

Box cover, pencil, ruler, scissors, matte knife, spray paint (optional).

Procedure

- First place the box cover on a sheet of drawing paper. Draw around it. This is the size of the drawing, so it will fit the frame.
- Measure three-quarters of the way up from the base of the box and draw a truncated pyramid. At the squared-off tip of the triangle draw a heavy line. This is scoring, so the cardboard will fold better.
- Cut the three sides with the matte knife; in the lower grades the teacher can easily do this. (Figure A)

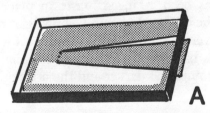

A

- Fold back and stand the frame up. (Figure B)
- The sides and back can be decorated with poster paints or quick-drying enamel spray can transform the ordinary box cover into a shiny, bright, stand-up frame.

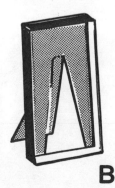

B

Lesson 7 Paper Sculpture Laurel Wreath Frame

Objectives

To create three-dimensional frames by a simple lesson in paper sculpture.

Materials

White drawing paper, scissors, pencil, white cardboard, glue.

Procedure

- First decide on the dimensions of the base and the shape. The one used here is a circular frame. Cut the cardboard into a circle 12″ in diameter.
- Draw a four-inch oval with a square base, and roll the point over a pencil. (Figure A)
- Cut thirty leaves, but before rolling and curling over the pencil, place them on the circular cardboard to get the proper effect. Start at the top and arrange the leaves one at a time at the edge, the right one slightly toward the center, and the left facing slightly outward. Continue down to the center base. When this has been arranged, paste in place. Do the same with the other side, again beginning at the top.
- Whatever art work is used, contrast it with a darker or lighter background. In the one in Figure B the background was darker and the art work lighter.

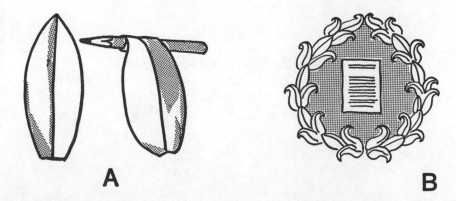

A   B

Lesson 8   Window Screening Stitchery Frame

Objectives

To use the art of stitchery on screening to make an unusual frame.

Materials

Window screening (modern, pliable, and soft, it can be bought by the yard at hardware stores), scissors, thick embroidery needle, embroidery thread or yarn, paper for design ideas.

Procedure

- Learn and practice the simple chain stitch of which there are numerous varieties. Design some easy flowers with this stitch. The first chain stitch is shown in close-up in Figure A1. Figure A2 illustrates a chain of these stitches. The blanket stitch is shown in Figure A3.

- Cut two pieces of 14" x 16" window screening; this will leave a 2" margin on top and sides and a 3" margin at the bottom edge. Place a 9" x 12" paper over the screening and run a thread around this picture size. (Figure B)

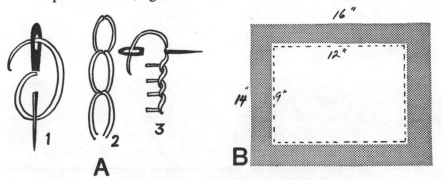

- Also run a thread of neutral color around the outside edges to hold the two pieces firmly in place while creating designs with embroidery thread.

- When the flowers or geometric shapes have been sewn on, use a blanket stitch and heavier yarn to finish off the edges. (Figure C)

Lesson 9   Coat Hanger and Wallpaper Frame

Objectives

Coat hangers are easily available and wallpaper stores often give away old wallpaper books, so this lesson is expense-free. While coat hangers are used in art classes as armatures and for sculpture, they can also become a different type of frame.

Materials

Lightweight coat hanger, wallpaper, waterproof glue, scissors, drawing paper, waxed paper.

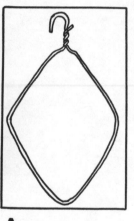

Procedure

- Stretch the coat hanger into the shape you want. (Figure A)
- Place the hanger on the drawing paper and draw around it to make a pattern of the exact size. Decide on an appropriate design for the edge. It can be a combination of straight and scalloped edges as illustrated in Figure B, or any other design you wish.
- Now place your pattern on the wallpaper and cut it out.

- Have plenty of newspaper on the table, because waterproof glue is difficult to remove. On the newspaper, add a sheet of waxed paper.
- Run a line of glue on the hanger and place the wallpaper pattern over it. Immediately press it with a weight and let it set.
- When dry, it is ready to display art work. A revolving frame can be made simply by covering both sides and letting it hang from the ceiling.

Lesson 10 Embossed Foil Frame

Objectives

Although tooling foil is expensive, art work made from it is durable and effective. However, you can also use ordinary aluminum foil for this project.

Materials

Household aluminum foil, cardboard, pencil, scissors, waterproof cement, ruler.

Procedure

- Decide on the size of drawing paper. If a 9″ x 12″ paper is preferred, cut a cardboard frame so it has a 2″ or 3″ border.
- Cut an opening somewhat smaller than the drawing, such as 8″ x 11″.
- Place the cardboard frame on the smoothed-out foil and gently draw around it and also around the opening.
- Cut off the corners on the dotted lines and cut the diagonal lines in the opening. (Figure A)
- Fold the center pieces back over the cardboard frame and bring the extra foil around the frame forward. (Figure B)
- Turn the frame over and plan your design. The slightest pressure will leave an imprint, so work

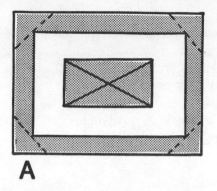

A

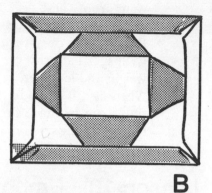

B

carefully pressing your design into the foil without tearing it. Use a ruler to draw around the edges and for diagonal lines from the corners to the opening. This will give the appearance of a real frame. Use scallops, lines, dots, and so on for decoration. (Figure C)

C

- Tape a piece of art work to the back of the frame and display proudly!

Bonus Ideas

Double Paper Plate Hanging Frames

Glue the rims of two paper plates together, but first decide on the shape of the opening, either square or circular. Punch a hole in the rim and secure a string. Cut two more plates with a different opening and glue together. Punch a hole at the base of the first set and the second at the top. Leave an inch between them and join. These hanging frames will move freely in different directions.

Bottle Cap Frames

By resorting to the classroom scrap box, all kinds of unusual frames can be made. Decide on basic frame and glue bottle caps in a neat row all around the edge. Glue the top of the cap onto the frame so the inside shows a fluted edge. Spray gold.

Shadow Box Frames

Two identical boxes are needed; however, experimentation will result in other ideas. Place the side of one box against the top of the other, repeat with another set of boxes. This will be a four-view frame displaying four pictures or three-dimensional piece of art work.

Play-Doh Relief Frames

Select a shallow box. Roll the Play-Doh into a definite shape—little squares, ovals, or balls and arrange around the edge evenly. Hand paint or spray the whole box silver. Place drawing, nature-study find, or picture in center.

Lace Doily and Cardboard Frame

Cut small white, silver, or gold lace doilies in half. Make a cardboard frame to hold 12" x 18" drawing. Arrange the half doilies at the inside edge so the scalloped edges are outside.

Contac Paper Frames

Contac paper is excellent to work with in all grades. First, no paste or glue is needed; and second, the left-over scraps can be used for endless collage motifs. Cut the frame from lightweight cardboard. Place the frame on the wrong side of the Contac paper and draw an inch larger on the outside and inside. At the eight corners, inside and outside, cut slits to the cardboard frame. Gently peel off the backing, place the cardboard on the sticky side, and fold over 1".

Hanging Oriental Frames

Select a sheet of long, panel-shaped white paper. Roll top and bottom edge over a large knitting needle. Slip a long, barkless branch through the top roll; add tassels and a string from either end of stick to hang it up.

Fabric Frames

Using the cardboard frame base, select a brightly patterned material and cover as with the Contac paper. Mount this on white drawing paper 1" wider than the total frame. Leave a half-inch space on the inside and contain the picture within the smaller lines.

Accordion-Fold Cylinder Frames

On 12" x 18" white paper plan an appropriately shaped opening in the center. With neatness and accuracy, begin accordion folding the entire sheet. Join into cylinder. Tape small picture inside.

Yarn Braided Frames

Braid bulky, brightly colored yarns loosely and glue or staple to a large oval paper plate. Glue the picture inside, leaving a white border.

CHAPTER 10

Exciting Box Ideas

*B*oxes are everywhere in all shapes and sizes. With the wide range of possibilities they offer, they make excellent materials for classroom art projects.

Collecting the boxes will not be difficult since the children enjoy being responsible for obtaining their own. The teacher can also keep an eye out for the particular types she wants and will eventually have enough for the idea she has in mind. The boxes can be stacked neatly inside each other until the day of the lesson.

From the teacher's example, the children will learn to be resourceful in hunting for boxes, planning ahead for the special project they would like to create.

Lesson 1   House of Windmills

Objectives

Cutting and bending skills are reviewed when children make windmills.

Materials

Lightweight poster paper of various colors, scissors, one quart or half-gallon empty milk carton, long straight pins, sand, glue, stapler, quick-drying spray paint.

Procedure

- Make a newspaper spray booth. Rinse out the milk carton and spray with paint.
- Fill three-quarters full with sand and glue the top, leaving two parts of the spout flared out. (Figure A)

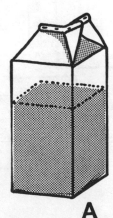

A

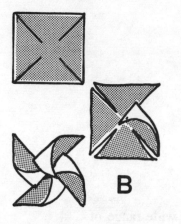

- Make many sizes of colored windmills. (Figure B)
- Poke small holes where the windmills can turn without touching each other and apply a little glue. Insert the windmills on the carton. (Figure C)
- Place where the air currents will cause a House of Turning Windmills.

B

C

Lesson 2   Decorative Flying Fish

Objectives

To stimulate the imagination by considering the potentials of a certain box shape, and by changing it into a decoration.

Materials

Vertical boutique tissue box with cellophane protective opening, scraps of red paper, glue, marker, 9″ x 12″ construction paper, needle and thread.

Procedure

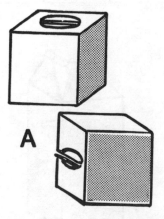

A

- A tissue box that is free from advertising is ideal for this project. Cut two red oval shapes from paper and glue onto the cellophane opening for the mouth. (Figure A)
- From black construction paper cut two large eyelids; make them long and deep enough to fringe eyelashes.

Curl these over a pencil. Draw an eye on each side of the box with a marker and glue eyelids over it.

- Add scales with the marker, cut decorative fins and tail, and glue on.
- With the long needle sew thread through each corner of the box and suspend to let the fish fly in the air. (Figure B)

B

Lesson 3 Penguin Bookends or Door Stopper

Objectives

To stylize a bird or animal with ready-made boxes.

Materials

One-quart milk container; spray paint; orange, white, and black paper; scissors; acrylic paints (optional); glue; sand; stapler.

Procedure

- Rinse carton thoroughly with warm, soapy water. Let it dry.
- Pull out the spout and fill the box three-quarters full with sand. Glue the top together and staple to keep the sand from seeping out if it is knocked over.
- Measure black paper so it covers the back and half of each side. Curve the side flippers so they stand slightly away from the box. Cut an oval shape from black paper for the tail and glue in place.
- Since it is a stylized bird, simply cut two oval feet and glue under the front of the box.
- With a marker draw a sharp, small eye on each side of the carton. The penguin is ready to guard your books or hold the door open! (Figure A)

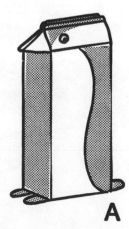

A

Lesson 4   Vanity Box

Objectives

To make a practical item through creative combination of variously shaped boxes.

Materials

A box about 8″ x 10″ with a top flap opening, smaller box with a lift-off top, a ribbon bow, small round mirror, glue, crayons or paint.

Procedure

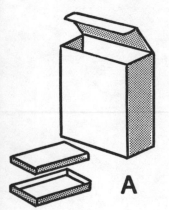

A

- Select the two boxes, one with a top flap opening, and a smaller box with a lift-off top. (Figure A)
- Close the flap of the large box, and lay it down so that the flap can be opened downward. Glue the bottom of the small box on the center of the large box. Glue the top of the small box standing up on its side at one end of the large box. (Figure B)
- Place the combination of boxes in a spray booth and paint it the color of your choice. Let dry.
- Glue a small mirror on the back of the vertical small box cover.
- Adhere a bow or a left-over rosette on the front flap of the large box as a decoration and also as a knob to open it. (Figure C)
- You now have a vanity to hold combs, hairpins, and small treasures!

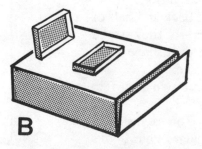

B

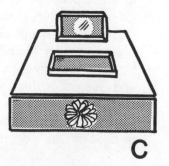

C

Lesson 5 Shake a Dry Snowstorm

Objectives

Use old Christmas cards to make a three-dimensional scene—a fun seasonal project.

Materials

Small box with ready-made cellophane opening, old Christmas cards, scissors, glue, artificial snow or soap flakes, white or pastel spray paint. If spray paint is not desired, cover the box with paper instead.

Procedure

A

- Protect the cellophane opening by covering it with a small piece of paper. Place it in the spray booth and paint a desired color.
- From old Christmas cards cut a tall tree and bright red house or a church. Leave a small tab at the bottom to be folded so the tree and house can be glued in place to stand up. Place one in back of the other for a three-dimensional effect. (Figure A)
- Cut out a distant hill scene and glue to the back of the box.
- Let it dry thoroughly and then place a small amount of snow flakes inside the box. Glue the top down and hold in place with a rubber band or string until set. Remove and the fun snowstorm is ready to begin! (Figure B)

B

Lesson 6 Musical Instruments

Objectives

To create instruments for the musical rhythm bands popular in the lower grades.

Materials

Clean frozen food trays, boxes, oval covers from plastic containers, small bells, string, pariscraft, scissors, narrow and wide rubber bands, spray paint (optional), cardboard tube.

Procedure

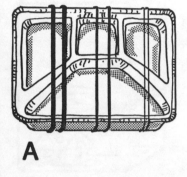

- The simplest musical instrument with a variety of sounds is the frozen food tray. Clean and dry the empty container. Then simply stretch both wide and narrow elastic bands around it at different intervals and begin to strum. (Figure A)

A

- A cereal box is ideal for the next instrument. Cut a circle in the center of the box; paint by hand or spray paint. Stretch elastic around the box over the opening. Add a handle of cardboard tubing from a paper towel roll. Cut slits at the base of the cardboard tube and glue in place. Let it dry and it's ready for fun! (Figure B)

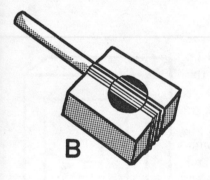

- A shake-the-bells instrument can be made from plastic container covers. Spray paint the cover, punch holes at intervals around the perimeter, and attach the bells with string through the holes. Shake for a gay tune! (Figure C)

B

- The square maraca is fun, too. Cover or spray a box. Inside put a small amount of uncooked popcorn kernels. Glue the cover shut. Cover a stick with pariscraft and firmly secure it to the box. Decorate and join in with the other music-makers! (Figure D)

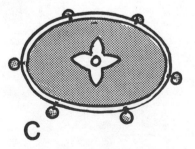

C

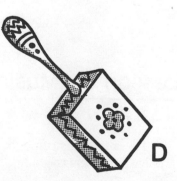

D

Lesson 7   Coat Hanger Box Tray

Objectives

Trays are always needed, especially at party time. This one is easy to make and need not be saved if space is scarce.

Materials

Two easy-to-bend coat hangers, shallow box cover or base, colored yarn, scissors.

A

Procedure

- Take a coat hanger and bend it into the position as illustrated in Figure A.
- Do the same with the other one, and overlap the hooks. Wind them together with brightly colored yarn. Tie the base together.
- Stretch the hanger base so it fits the box cover. Poke two holes on opposite sides and secure the hanger and box with yarn. The box is ready for classroom party time! (Figure B)

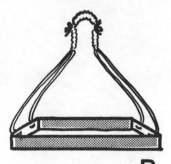

B

Lesson 8   Lollipop Centerpiece

Objectives

To invent ideas for classroom parties or at-home decorations with no cost but time and imagination.

Materials

A variety of clean boxes, glue, colored construction paper or spray paint, and, of course, lollipops.

Procedure

- Select three boxes that, when placed one on top of the other, make a good proportion.

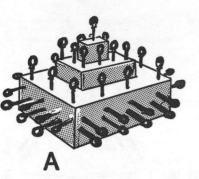

A

- You can make the tops of the boxes one color and the sides another, or simply glue them together and spray paint.
- In Figure A the sides were covered with brightly colored construction paper and the top had a lighter color. The boxes were then glued in place, one on top of the other.
- When dry, the lollipops were placed on a preplanned arrangement. A small hole was first pierced and the candy sticks pushed through. What a colorful arrangement of goodies for a treat!

Lesson 9 Classroom Store-all

Objectives

Every classroom has a need for extra rulers, brushes, and other materials, so this lesson shows how to make a store-all.

Materials

Two empty one-quart milk containers, glue, scraps of colored construction paper, sand, stapler, marker, one-half pint cream container.

Procedure

A

- Rinse out the three dairy containers with warm, soapy water.
- Open the tops of the milk containers completely and glue them together side by side; staple the adjoining sides together at the top.
- Fill each of the milk containers three-quarters full of sand to weight them down. Spray paint the exterior.
- Cut five feathers out of construction paper and color with bright designs. Staple these at the back of the cartons. Cut a strip of construction paper for the headband and decorate. Glue in place. With a marker add eyes and nose.
- The empty cream container can be added at the center of the base of the milk cartons to form a

mouth with a mustache of paintbrushes sticking out of the sand inside. (Figure A)
- Try your hand at arranging a milk-container design of efficient storage boxes.

Lesson 10 Stretchable Scrapbook or Picture Book

Objectives

It's fun to make a different kind of picture book and here is one that is stretchable. It can be seen easily by many pupils and stands alone for all to view.

Materials

Shallow box with lift-off cover, construction paper, crayons or magazine clippings, glue, and scissors.

Procedure

- Select a strong, clean box with a lift-off cover.
- Measure the inside of the box cover using the bottom of the box.
- Plan as many pages as you wish; however, eight is a good number since after the gluing of the first page a total of fourteen pictures can be seen. (Figure A)
- After the pages have been cut and folded, plan the theme and decide whether drawings or clippings are to be used.
- When the art work is finished, assemble the book by gluing the first and last page onto the covers. (Figure B)

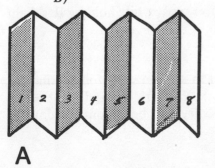

A

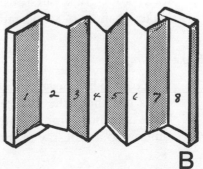

B

- The pages can be folded back into the book when not needed or stretched out to stand for all to see.

This does not necessarily have to be used for art work, but possibly for the fourteen best spelling papers for a P.T.A. night display.

Bonus Ideas

Desk Caddy

The cereal package containing ten small varieties is ideal for a desk caddy. When the packages are empty, try rearranging them to hold pencils, markers, stamps, clips, and erasers. Stand the boxes upright in the center of the tray; lay the side ones flat with open tops. When glued and dry, spray paint the entire caddy for strength and appearance.

Seasonal Box Tree

Collect many sizes of boxes. Experiment with them in building a tree, larger ones at the bottom ending with a small thin one at top. Glue and spray paint. This tree can be used for Easter eggs, Christmas ornaments, or small craft work.

Totem Pole Box Post

Study totem pole carvings. Collect boxes about the same width and determine the height needed. Fill with sand and glue cover to base. When all boxes are assembled and glued to form a post, paint the symbols of a clan.

Halloween Flashlight Box

Cereal boxes are easy to cut. Open top and remove flaps. Cut square openings on each side and line with orange crepe paper using waterproof glue. Cut features out of black paper and glue in place. Make a handle of string and dangle over wrist while holding flashlight inside.

Egg Seedling Box

Select any shape egg box and line each section with foil, fluting the edges just above the surface of the box. Fill with soil and plant seeds. Make a handle out of the cover. Carry the box from window to window so it will stay in the sunshine.

Bird-House Box

Four not-too-shallow boxes are required: one for the base, one for the top, and two for side ends. Glue with waterproof glue and spray paint for outdoor protection. Place seeds in tray.

Tiny Box Place Cards

Glue the cover of the box backwards at the end of the base. Letter the name of your guest and put small candies in a plastic bag and tie with bright ribbon.

Macaroni Mosaic Box

Select flat shapes of macaroni and arrange in an original design at the center of the box, radially extending the design to the sides. Use waterproof glue and spray paint in your favorite colors.

Box Robot

Eight boxes will make the basic figure of a person. Glue all together except for the arms, which are long boxes with no elbow joint. Use fasteners for these so they can swing back and forth. Paint this robot gay colors, or spray silver.

Handy Telephone Caddy

Make either a wall or desk caddy, selecting the size and shape of the boxes according to the space allotted. Glue a pad of paper to the base box, add a loop of paper to hold a pencil with a string attached and a small calendar.

CHAPTER 11

Lively Posters

Posters came into existence with the development of the printing press during the fifteenth century, but only became recognized as a form of art in this century. A good poster is one that includes bold colors, simple design, and a clear, brief message that is free of details. Posters can be an excellent classroom activity simply because of the many events, seasonal and otherwise, that arise during the school year.

Posters can be of any size depending on their purpose. They provide an effective learning experience either as an individualized lesson in the classroom or as a large-scale community project. Motivation for poster projects comes from an endless array of sources: school plays, fashion shows, art exhibits, P.T.A. nights, science fairs, field trips, or movies. They provide a prime opportunity to use imagination and inventiveness.

Lesson 1   Revolving Lampshade Poster

Objectives

The new teacher can introduce himself with this unusual lamp poster that illustrates his interests. For friendly inter-action, each child can make and display his own lamp poster.

Materials

A lamp with a big shade and a heavy, sturdy base, clippings cut from magazines, snapshots, glue, scissors, marker, a band of colored construction paper.

Procedure

• The teacher, by having his lamp poster displayed,

motivates his pupils to begin planning one of their own either at home or in school.

- Measure a wide band of colored paper to encircle the shade.
- Arrange snapshots in time sequence across the strip. Glue in place, wrap around the shade, and tape ends together.
- With a marker, letter the name of the teacher and the grade.
- The lamp poster, shown in Figure A, introduces the children to their new teacher in a friendly and informative way.
- Some children may bring in a lampshade and make a story of themselves—a "Me" poster that revolves.

A

Lesson 2   Health and Ecology Posters

Objectives

Principles of good health and ecology should be stressed often with young children. Through poster art they can become aware of their role in these important areas.

Materials

Large piece of oaktag or cardboard, empty school milk carton, straw, magazine clippings, colored construction paper, small brown lunch bag, scissors, glue, marker, paints.

Procedure

- Begin with the health poster. Draw your message in large block letters at least 4" tall and three-quarters of an inch wide on brightly colored paper. Cut them out.
- Paste or staple a sheet of contrasting paper to the cardboard or oaktag. Apply the message in an attractive design.
- Cut some pictures of health foods from magazines.
- Rinse out a small school milk carton with warm, soapy water. Let it dry. Insert a straw.

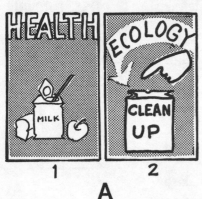

A

• Create a design of your own arrangement using the carton. (Figure A1)
• Ecology posters can have a message and at the same time be functional. Figure A2 shows a poster with a clean-up bag attached to it.
• For the ecology poster select a brightly colored paper for the background and glue it over the cardboard, or use a sheet of poster board in a lively color. Plan a band of a light color and letter the word *Ecology*.
• Glue the paper bag in place and you have a useful classroom display.

Lesson 3 Seasonal P.T.A. Posters

Objectives

P.T.A. nights are important events. Children can make posters that remind parents that a special time has been set aside for them.

Materials

Large poster board of 12″ x 18″ paper of a bright seasonal color, three paper plates, macaroni shells or bows, glue, bands of other colored construction paper, marker or paints.

Procedure

A

• Have some children cut large, bright letters "P.T.A.".
• Glue a single letter on each plate. Color the edge of the plate with a seasonal design.
• Ask other children to help decorate the edge of the poster with macaroni bows, shells, or other shapes. Glue these in place.
• Cut bands of paper in appropriate colors and letter the month and date, plus a friendly *Welcome* for all parents. Encourage children to discuss arrangement of the parts to make the poster. (Figure A)

Lesson 4 · Reusable Birthday Poster

Objectives

In the elementary grades, a birthday is a special event and deserves recognition. A basically designed birthday poster can be used over and over again by simply changing the names.

Materials

Large sheet of paper or poster board, colored construction paper, small artificial flowers or those cut from magazines, paste, strip of black construction paper, markers, wide flat container, small birthday candles, white blackboard chalk.

Procedure

- Plan the background with gay pastel colors: blue paper with a pink border, yellow with green, etc.
- Letter *Happy Birthday to* in big letters with a marker.
- Cut a strip of black construction paper any size to letter on (5" x 12" is a good size).
- Staple the small artificial flowers or cut flowers from magazines for a festive decoration.
- Wrap brightly colored paper around a wide, short flower pot or container and fill with sand. Place on a table pushed up to the bulletin board.
- If it is Jimmie's birthday, let him write his own name with white chalk on the black paper, then tape it to the poster.
- Let Jimmie put the appropriate number of candles into the sand. Light them (if school allows it). Sing the birthday song to Jimmie. (Figure A)

A

Lesson 5   Changeable Twelve-month Calendar

Objectives

The classroom usually has a corner ideal for a stand-up calendar. Here is an opportunity to place children's drawings pertaining to a particular month. Change art work often, giving each child a chance to see his work displayed.

Materials

Two large poster boards or sheets of plain cardboard (sometimes grocery stores have old posters to give away), strips of cardboard, shallow box cover that is a little larger than paper used, masking tape, marker.

Procedure

- Cover the cardboard with white paper for all seasons.
- Cut a strip of paper of any size; letter the month *September.* Roll masking tape sticky side out and tack onto background.
- Take the shallow box cover and glue it onto the poster.
- Make a support to hold the tent open, so the two sides will stand firmly without spreading.
- As the drawings are created during the month of September, there can be a constant changing of pupils' work, so each one will have a chance to show his picture separately. (Figure A)

A

Lesson 6 Current Events Poster

Objectives

Even in the lower grades children are aware of daily happenings in the world. Children will bring in clippings from newspapers on sports, trips to the moon, art, music, and other events. To encourage this interest a "Current Events" poster can become a classroom project.

Materials

Sheet of 18" x 24" white paper, single sheet of newspaper, paste (wallpaper paste is good), scissors, marker or precut letters, cardboard backing, news clippings, wide house paintbrush.

Procedure

- With a wide house paintbrush spread wallpaper paste over the sheet of white paper. Place the single page of newspaper over it and smooth out.
- Plan the size of the opening and draw with pencil first, while paste is damp.
- Cut carefully from the center to the size of the opening and curl these pieces over a pencil; pull the pencil out, and let the curved paper dry.
- Paste this sheet onto a cardboard backing or tack it on the bulletin board. Mark *News* or *Current Events* at the top. Roll pieces of masking tape sticky side out and tack items inside the opening.
- Keep the news changing to encourage children's interest. (Figure A)

A

Lesson 7 All-purpose Mailbox Poster

Objectives

There are numerous occasions in the classroom where a mailbox idea can be utilized. There are opportunities to send cards to and from classmates: a sick child, to one who had an accident, to one who is going away, on Valentine's Day, and many others. With a central decorative poster to collect the mail, children can enjoy greeting-card art activity while learning about human relations.

Materials

Large poster board or large paper tacked to bulletin board, cereal or cookie box with open top flap, markers, colored construction paper.

Procedure

A

- If this poster is to be on the bulletin board, staple a large sheet of white paper to the board. Staple a brightly colored piece of construction paper in the center to allow a 2″ white border around the sides.
- Using a different colored marker for each side, letter *Happy Birthday, Going Away?, Get Well Soon, Be My Valentine,* or other ideas the class may want. (Figure A)
- With a black marker letter the word *Mailbox* on the front of the box. Staple this box to the bulletin board or glue it on.
- When all the letters have been written and placed in the mailbox, remove them, package in one envelope, and send them to the remembered classmate.

Lesson 8 Wallpaper and
Pipe Cleaner Posters

Objectives

Discarded wallpaper books can give a new look to posters. Each class member can be represented by an original wallpaper and pipe-cleaner flower in a communal poster project. This theme is ideal for a spring art exhibition.

Materials

Large sheet of white paper to be tacked onto bulletin board, small print wallpaper, pipe cleaners, paste, paints or colored markers.

Procedure

- Have children make big, wide letters on practice paper first.
- After selecting a small, bright pattern in the wallpaper book, place the letters upside down and trace around them. Or, if it isn't too difficult to see the pencil lines, place them right side up on the pattern.
- Cut them out neatly and try arranging them in various ways: in horizontal, curved, and vertical lines. Paste them on the paper.
- Have the children invent different shapes for flowers, keeping the petals all in one flat piece. Cut a different-colored wallpaper for flat centers. Bend the pipe cleaner in a small hook and tape onto the back of the blossom.
- Arrange them at the bottom of the poster and staple or tape in place. Bend them slightly forward. Add green wallpaper for grass.
- Letter with a marker *Art Exhibition.*
- The show is ready to begin with this gay poster! (Figure A)

A

Lesson 9 Pet Puzzle Poster

Objectives

This is an unusual poster project in which the children can put a puzzle together and at the same time be reminded to take good care of their pets. The cover can only be put on the box if the puzzle is correctly put in place and the pet is safe and sound.

Materials

Large piece of cardboard, an easy animal puzzle, glue, markers.

Procedure

- First, draw around the box to determine how much room will be left for large lettering, since a good poster should contain clear, large words.
- Letter your message.
- Glue the bottom of the box in place and let set to dry. (Figure A)
- Rest the cardboard on a stack of books or a box, remove the cover, take out the puzzle pieces and the game poster is ready.
- What an easy poster to have fun with and at the same time teach a good message about pets! (Figure B)

A

B

Lesson 10 Halloween Round Poster

Objectives

It's fun to have a different dimension poster in the classroom—a poster that can be moved about and at the same time not take up too much space.

Materials

18" x 24" sheet of black construction paper, orange construction paper, scissors, small scraps of orange and white paper, paste, stapler, white pencil or white chalk.

Procedure

A

- Cut a 3" strip of orange paper 24" long.
- Holding the black paper horizontally, roll into a cylinder only overlapping about one inch. Staple together. If the stapler doesn't reach all the way down the side, add some glue.
- To find the width of the lettering wrap the orange strip around the black cylinder and mark at the diameter. Then letter *Halloween* in black.
- Cut large white eyes and color in black for pupils.
- Cut a wide triangle of black paper and glue or staple at the top, just over the eyes.
- Cut an oval of orange paper for his beak. Add claws of orange paper also. The poster is ready to announce the coming Halloween party. (Figure A)

Bonus Ideas

Field Trip Poster-Bulletin Board

Set aside one end of the bulletin board for this poster. Use shallow boxes to display separate themes. The oak tree and its nut, the shell and its habitat, and the flower and its season are possible themes. Label the theme with big letters.

Paper Sculpture Poster

Any sculpture can involve paper sculpture. For autumn, original leaves curled and stapled to branches make a bright and different poster. A spring art show can boast paper-sculpture flowers.

Clean Hands Poster

Draw around the hands, right and left, on clean white paper. Add fingernails. Curl the fingers slightly for a realistic effect and mount on blue construction paper. Title: *Clean Hands.*

Vacation Postcard Posters

Have children bring in postcards of their trips. Clip the cards with paper clips and secure threads to each. Cover the bulletin board with white paper or make a large poster board. Cut big letters for the word *Vacation,* and suspend a card from each letter. Change the cards every so often.

Tent Corridor Posters

Cut two large corrugated boards and join at the top to make a tent; staple a strip of cardboard at the base to sides at even distance. For a movie poster cut letters out of old negatives. Cut black and white photos to form a vertical column that resembles a filmstrip.

Famous Art Prints Poster

Select a famous artist's reproduction appropriate for the month. Letter the name of the artist in big letters. Select various pieces of material to match textures in the picture. Cut these into forms representative of the subject matter—flowers for Van Gogh's *Sunflowers,* for example. Arrange these flowers in a large V shape and paste the print over it.

Double Coat Hanger Posters

Here is a poster that can be hung up in a minute. Spray the hanger any color or leave it as is. Cut two large sheets of paper just the width of the bar. Plan the poster theme and staple at the top so a poster hangs on each side.

Mobile Posters

Design a mobile having the title in large block letters, joined to make a single unit. Study novelty lettering in magazines. Balance the word with separate pictures hanging by threads to create a pleasing mobile. Both sides should be alike.

Perception Box Poster

Select a large, deep box. Paste pictures on the inside. Have each wall of the box depict a different idea with a one-word title. Then make a small hole in the walls of the box to peer through.

Standing Three-Dimensional Tree Poster

Sometimes a decorative, informative display is desired and a 36″ tall triangle works well. Cut three triangles, tape the sides together, and add poster news. Set on top of a bucket, tape tree to a container.

CHAPTER 12

Creative Construction Ideas

*C*hildren are fascinated with construction projects. Mixed media can be used as materials, or use a single item in various sizes, colors, and textures. The freedom and creativity involved attract the timid child as well as the self-motivated one in attempting original projects.

The older levels can discuss the importance of space relationship, called negative spaces; and the design of objects in harmony with each other, called positive spaces. Design of the total construction and the elements required for a pleasing result include balance, unity, movement, direction, and a visual center. All of these suggestions can result in interaction between teacher and pupil, with emphasis on the child's perception.

Lesson 1   Thread, Cardboard, and Paper Plates

Objectives

Ordinary sewing thread is easy to handle and provides a way of discovering color combinations by making decorative paper-plate designs.

Materials

Various colored spools of sewing-machine thread, cardboard shapes, paper plates, scissors, glue.

Procedure

- Prepare different shapes of cardboard in various colors—triangular, square, circular, freeform, or oval.

- On one side cut two slots, on the opposite side cut eight slots.
- Tie a knot at the end of the thread and insert in one slot of the two-slot side. Holding the spool in the left hand, lead the thread in front of the cardboard around slot "B" into slot "C" and back to "A." (Figure A) Keep the thread on the front side only if it is to be mounted. If it is to become part of a mobile where both sides are seen, wind thread around the entire shape.
- Try an angular shape with a center cut out. Wind the thread over the opening for a different effect. (Figure B)
- Experiment with the three primary colors, red, yellow, and blue. In this thread design, the colors will overlap creating three new colors: green (blue and yellow); violet (red and blue); orange (red and yellow). (Figure C)
- Cut slots along the edge of a paper plate and try a radial design. (Figure D) This will lead to other experiments.

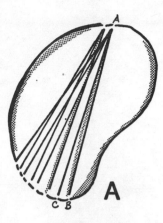

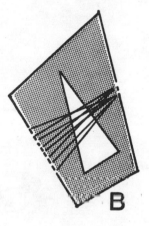

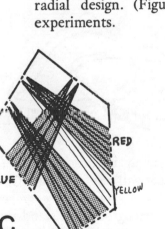

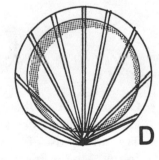

Lesson 2 Möbius Strip Designs— Topology

Objectives

Here is a chance for art and mathematics to be related. The Möbius strip is a one-sided surface formed from a rectangular strip of paper by rotating one end 180 degrees, and attaching it to the other end. The inventor was the German mathematician, August Möbius (1790-1868).

Materials

Paper, scissors, pencil, glue, spray paint.

Procedure

- Cut a strip of paper 1½″ wide and 18″ long. Mark letter "A" on one end, turn strip over and mark "B" on the other end. (Figure A) Turn end marked "B" over until both "A" and "B" are side by side. Glue together.
- Starting at "A," draw a pencil line all around the strip until "B" is reached. Cut on that line and watch for the surprise. Suddenly you will have two circles interlocked! (Figure B)

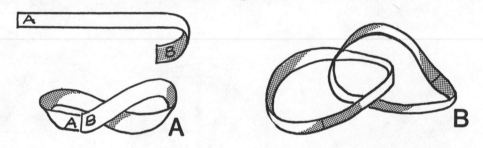

- Cut only one of these circles again through the center and three interlocked circles will result. (Figure C)
- Try all kinds of arrangements with these graceful forms. Mount them on a background or stand them up with a cardboard support on a base. Spray lightly with quick-drying enamel spray.

Lesson 3   Tacks, Corkboard, and Thread

Objectives

To explore color in line and overlapping directions using tacks and left-over corkboard. A multitude of interesting patterns results from simple geometric shapes. Again, combining art and mathematics is a fun project for all children.

Materials

Corkboard, tacks, sewing thread, scissors, glue, poster paints.

Procedure

- Select a piece of corkboard and make a paper pattern the same size. On the paper plan the design; when the idea is formed, darken with a soft pencil using a ruler, since the end result will be straight lines.
- For the first three-dimensional design, start with lines drawn from corner to corner to find the center. Shade the center and add a small, black rectangle for a vanishing-point effect.
- On the diagonal lines space tacks; the tacks should be close together near the center and get farther apart until the corner is reached. (Figure A)
- For the next design draw two circles, the smaller one near the center and a larger circumference near the edge. Place tacks in this design. Tie thread around the tacks, using your own color combinations. (Figure B)
- For the third pattern a square was started in the center first. Inside a silhouette of a man was painted. The groups of threads on each side of the square are in the same color and the remaining ones contrast with them. (Figure C)

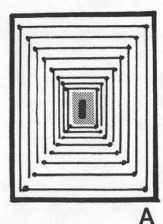

A

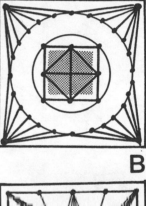

B

C

Lesson 4 Straws and Pipe Cleaner Forms

Objectives

Straws are easy to obtain and inexpensive. They vary in size, color, and design, and hence offer much creative opportunity. Pipe cleaners are also an easily available item. Experiments with them can be endless. They can be reworked over and over again. From geometric shapes to imaginary animals all become fun search lessons with these materials.

Materials

Straws (including flex-straws), pipe cleaners, scissors.

Procedure

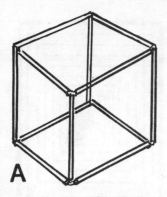

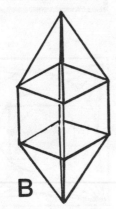

- By cutting straws in half for the first lessons, each child can have his own supply within easy reach. With a handful of pipe cleaners he is ready to begin.
- Try making a cube; strive for square corners and a cube that will stand flat on the desk. (Figure A)
- Add more pipe cleaners by inserting them into the corners to make a pointed top. Do this on the base also. (Figure B)
- While the straight straws are fun to work with, the flex-straw with its bending quality can easily be turned into animals. Imaginary animals made with flex-straws offer a great deal of freedom in construction. (Figure C)
- *Note*—The average package of straws contains 100 about 8″ long. The jumbo-sized flex-straws have forty per box. Combine them for variations in size and color.

A

B

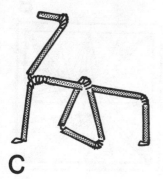

C

Lesson 5   Pariscraft Macramé

Objectives

This is a good lesson in which to make use of pariscraft scraps, and at the same time not involve a large project. It is a way to become acquainted with the potentials of this material.

Materials

Pariscraft, water, scissors, waxed paper, newspapers, branch, masking tape.

Procedure

- Secure waxed paper to the table at the four corners.
- Tape this down. The waxed paper and branch can be taped at the same time, this is optional.
- Cut six strips of pariscraft and have ready. Create your designs and knots after this first introduction.
- Dip a strip in the water and when limp wrap around the branch, spacing them evenly across the branch. (Figure A)
- Don't try knots right away, just overlap two at a time always keeping the strips separate so they won't stick together. Overlap the first three sets; alternate on the second row. This will leave the outside strip hanging alone. Tape it in place until it dries to form the same space as the overlapped ones. (Figure B)
- Repeat this pattern until you have the length that is pleasing.
- This lace work should dry in ten to fifteen minutes. When ready, lift off the waxed paper and hang unadorned or later interlace with brightly colored bulky yarns or ribbon.

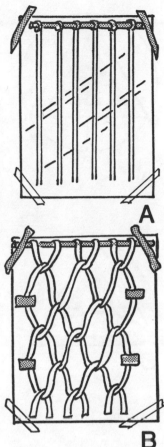

Lesson 6   Icosahedron Form

Objectives

For an older group, learning how to construct an equilateral triangle is interesting. They will learn how to score, fold, and assemble a twenty-sided figure. Once this is assembled it can be used for a seasonal holiday decoration. It can be also used in parts for hats, baskets, or centerpieces. It holds many possibilities for designing.

Materials

Construction paper, scissors, ruler, compass, pencil.

Procedure

- It is a good idea for the teacher to refresh her memory in making an equilateral tirangle. A pattern

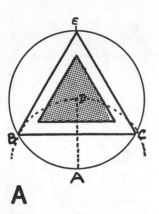

A

B

might be of advantage in some cases. Draw a circle of any size.

- Draw a radius from "A" to "D." Stretch the compass until it touches "A" to "D," then swing it to either side until it intercepts the circumference, "B" and "C."
- Draw a line using the ruler from "B" to "C." Holding the ruler on the radius make a mark at "E." Now construct the triangle. At this time draw a smaller triangle inside. Cut out. (Figure A)
- With the scissors open draw over lines "B" to "C" to "E." Then fold. The edges will be sharp and smooth. Cut the inside triangle out. (Figure B)
- Cut twenty circles, removing the center triangle and folding on the larger triangle.
- Plan the arrangement on the table first. For the top and base place the folded circle in a pie shape, five triangles to each pie.
- Place ten together in a row inverting every other triangle. (Figure C)

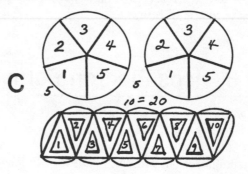

C

- Total them up: 5+5+10=20 pieces.
- Glue them together beginning with two pie pieces. Glue the flaps neatly. Glue the strip of ten together with flaps out also.
- Assemble the entire three-piece set: top, to middle band, to the base. Let the glue set. A perfect sphere should be formed. (Figure D)
- Tie a string at the top. Hang under a hall light to catch interesting patterns of light and shadow.
- Use seasonal colors in making the icosahedron. Hang a center cluster of Christmas ornaments inside, owl for Halloween, or an Easter egg for spring.
- For added glamour, glue sequins on the faces of the figure and it will sparkle as it slowly turns in the air

D

current. Colored tissue paper covering the openings is effective also.

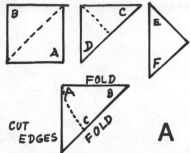

Lesson 7 Snowflake Constructions

Objectives

This lesson provides a review of folding and cutting paper to make snowflakes with creative adaptations.

Materials

Construction paper, scissors, boxes, candle and holder, glue, pencil, gold or silver spray (optional), thread or string.

Procedure

- Briefly review snowflake construction. Cut a square out of white paper. Fold corner "A" to corner "B." Fold "C" to "D." Fold "E" to "F."
- Measure the edge A-B and make C-B the same length. Cut off the excess past the dotted line. (Figure A)
- On the fold edges, cut out shapes leaving a paper fold between open areas. Also plan an interesting edge at the curved open side. (Figure B)
- Open the pattern and a snowflake will appear. (Figure C)
- Using these snowflake patterns of numerous designs cover a box with brightly colored paper. Glue the snowflakes on each side. Suspend the box and hang where all can watch it turn. (Figure D)
- Glue seven snowflakes on different colored paper and press until flat and stiff. Cut into the center of six of them and insert them together to make a stand-up assemblage.
- Pierce a hole in the center of four progressive sizes and slip over a candle for a snowflake tree.

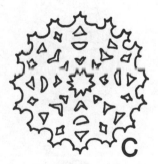

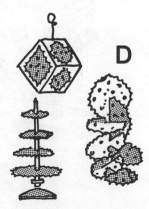

Lesson 8   Pariscraft Experiments

Objectives

Pariscraft is a delightful medium with which to work. Frequently scraps are left over that lend themselves to experimentation. In this lesson balloons and branches in combination with pariscraft show what unusual ideas can develop.

Materials

Pariscraft, water, scissors, balloons, branches, block of wood, box to be covered.

Procedure

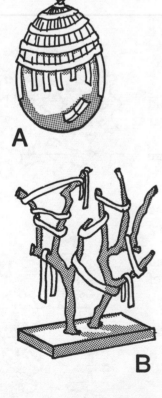

- Blow up a balloon and tie securely so the air will not escape. It must be tightly knotted or the weight of the wet pariscraft will force the air out.
- Tie a string to the neck of the balloon. Either set it in a bowl to prevent it from sliding around or hang it up within easy reach over plenty of newspapers.
- Cut many strips of pariscraft in different lengths and set aside.
- Begin at the top placing flat strips vertically down the sides of the balloon. When the balloon has been covered three-quarters of the way down, proceed to add the strips horizontally around the balloon. (Figure A) Pierce the balloon when dry and remove it. The form is ready to hang with an added center ornament.
- Find two branches and a box each in proportion to the other.
- Close the box, add sand for weight (optional). Push branches into the box. Cover with pariscraft, let dry until set. Experiment with lines, shapes, and hangings over the branches. (Figure B)

Lesson 9 Accordion-folded Paper Units

Objectives

If children learn to fold and cut paper the right way they will not be discouraged with the results. This is especially true of the older groups. There is nothing sharper and more beautiful than cleanly scored and folded white paper. Through creative cutting and shaping all sorts of abstract building units can be developed. When each child has made one single unit of his own creation, these can be assembled into a striking city complex.

Materials

White construction paper, scissors, ruler, pencil, black cardboard or construction paper for display, invisible tape.

Procedure

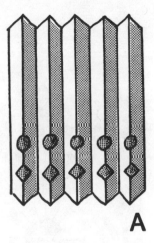

- For practice begin with a 9" x 12" piece of white paper. Mark off half inches all across the top and also on the bottom edge. Connect these lines with a ruler and pencil.
- Open the scissors and turn upside down. Again using the ruler, pull the scissor edge over the lines.
- Fold, beginning at the center, with the paper flat on the table. To do this use both hands at the center and fold by moving both hands away from each other out to the edges. Fold forward and backward. Stand it up in cylinder form and tape.
- Try cutting circles and triangles on the folds. (Figure A)
- Experiment with a variety of cuttings on the folds. Try cutting the top edge in a curve. (Figure B)

A

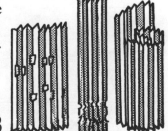

B

Lesson 10 Scrap Construction

Objectives

There are days when children should be given the challenge to create a theme with no one knowing what it is until it is ready for display. Using scrap materials is ideal for this activity. Left-over fabrics, bottle caps, toothpicks, plasticine, and endless materials found in the classroom collage box invite ideas. Each child is to make a creative construction having a definite theme in mind.

Materials

Contents of the collage box (a box every classroom should have that is constantly being depleted and replenished), scissors, glue.

Procedure

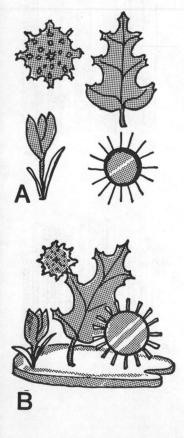

A

B

- Let each child choose a theme of his own. A list of possible themes may help out the few slow starters. Some of these might be: Nature, The Sea, The Farm House, Spring, Pilgrims, Holidays, My Home, or The Four Seasons.
- In the figures shown here The Four Seasons was chosen. Many symbols can be used to depict this idea, such as an oak leaf to symbolize autumn, a snowflake for winter, a metallic yellow paper sun with toothpicks as rays for summer, and a crepe-paper crocus for spring. (Figure A)
- The base of the display is made of plasticine cut in a freeform shape, the edge painted a neutral gray and the top white.
- Allow the children to create their own compositions for the elements of the display. Figure B illustrates the kind of balance of design the children should strive for.

Bonus Ideas

Ideas with Parts of Icosahedron

Refer back to lesson 6 in this chapter for the construction of this geometric form. The top pie-shaped part can be used as a hat or a hanging basket by tying strings at three points. This section can also be a centerpiece surrounded with a holiday theme and filled with seasonal items.

Dodecahedron (Twelve-Sided Figure)

Each face is a pentagon having five sides. Any 6th grader can make these once a pattern is established. Six sides are glued together for the top and six for the base, joined together they equal twelve in all. Hang the figure as a mobile. Each face can be decorated with sequins or colored crayons.

Abstract Toothpick Building Forms

Begin by constructing a variety of toothpick forms. Make two squares by gluing the ends together, placing the second one inside the first at an angle. Glue and dry. Make sunburst shapes, diamonds, lattices, etc. Glue these to spatulas, twigs, or craft sticks. Imbed in a square of plasticine and paint.

Paper Cup Growing Designs

Glue three paper cups onto an inverted box top. Have rims touching. Build up pyramid style; use waterproof glue. Use a larger cup for the first row and decrease in size as it grows in height. Leave empty, or add colorful, paper, abstract flowers or dry, lightweight branches.

Paper Plates and Straws

Collect paper plates of different colors and designs. Place one plate upside down on the table. Flatten ends of straws and glue around the edge for a sunburst design. Let dry; add a second plate using ample glue and press to set. Hang this one singly or add others so the spokes interweave. Use a theme and paste appropriate pictures in the centers of the plates.

Scrap Assemblage

Ask children to bring into class various discarded objects. These will be of many textures—a wheel from a toy car, balls in stages of disuse, branches, milk cartons, etc. Let them experiment with assembling a unit in a design they like.

Coat Hanger and Crepe Paper Shapes

Stretch two coat hangers and fit at angles to each other. Bind together with pipe cleaners. Wind the coat hangers with brightly colored crepe paper. Using crepe-paper streamers gather 12" lengths into circular shapes and staple. Suspend with threads to center of space. Simple flower forms can be made and attached around the frame.

Window Screening Forms

Explore shapes with window screening, creating a fish, a duck, or another favorite animal. Roll screening into a cone shape for the fish. Staple. Add fins and tail. Draw, cut, and color two large eyes; glue.

Plasticine and Pipe Cleaner Buildings

Start with a square of plasticine for main building. Roll clay to form columns, chimney stacks, fences, etc. Use pipe cleaners for thin additions such as telephone wires. Make an imaginary city unit.

Cardboard, Paper, and Yarn Construction

Cut different shaped openings in 9" x 12" pieces of cardboard. Cut two slits at one end and several at the opposite side. Wind yarn around the cardboard using one color. Keeping the two slots as the focal point, make a fan-shaped yarn pattern. Add other colors with a different set of cuts on the edges. Design shapes out of colored construction paper and weave in and out of the yarn. These could be abstract flower, animal, bird, or fish themes.

CHAPTER 13

Storybook Animal, Bird, and Fish Sculpture

$\mathcal{S}$culpture has three forms—bas-relief, high, and in the round. These forms are each used in their own right, or are sometimes combined in one piece of sculpture. With these possibilities, creativity in this medium is given full range.

Sculpture appeals to all ages, providing opportunities for both realistic and fantasy work. Classroom studies offer ideas for individual expression in sculpture, along with original ideas from the pupils themselves. The advance of new materials and the combination of known ones can challenge the pupils' inventiveness, tease their imaginations, and develop resourcefulness through research for their projects.

Lesson 1   Flat Papier-mâché Animal

Objectives

Flat papier-mâché is best handled with simple, easily cut designs, therefore an animal that is sturdily built lends itself to this medium well.

Materials

Plenty of newspaper, wide flat brush, wallpaper paste, scissors, poster paints or spray paint (optional).

Procedure

- Spread out newspaper on the work area. Get three

A

B

more sheets of newspaper, preferably from the financial section.

- Mix up the wallpaper paste. On the first sheet brush a coating of paste evenly over the entire page. Cover it immediately with the second sheet. Repeat with the third sheet. Smooth out any wrinkles.
- Draw the animal on the newspaper while it is still damp. Depending on the classroom project, patterns may have been previously cut out. Draw two animals. (Figure A)
- Press these animals flat and let dry. Paint or spray.
- To make the animal stand up, run paste along the top edge pasting together the tail and face. Leave ears and legs slightly apart. (Figure B)

Lesson 2 Balloon and Pariscraft Elephant

Objectives

Balloons make an excellent base for animal forms. This lesson might begin with a discussion comparing the East Indian and African elephants. However, the aim is not to reproduce them in sculpture, but rather use them as an introduction for some fun elephants.

Materials

Balloons, two cardboard tubes from towel rolls, pariscraft, scissors, water, newspapers.

Procedure

- Always cover the work table with newspaper when using pariscraft; it saves on cleanup.

- Blow up the small balloon and cover with strips of pariscraft. When dry remove the balloon. Do the same with the large balloon.
- Cut one cardboard tube into quarters; leave the other long.
- Cover the short tubes with pariscraft and then set the body of the elephant on top. For balance and support, be sure legs are far enough apart.
- Join the head to the body and immediately add the tube for the trunk. Let this rest on the table for added support. (Figure A)
- Cut construction paper ear patterns and cover. Join to head.
- Twist strips of pariscraft for a short tail and two tusks; join.
- Shape the trunk at the head and draw the nostril.
- When dry, paint the elephant, add eyes and toenails. He's ready for fun! (Figure B)

Lesson 3   Bottle and Pariscraft Animals

Objectives

The plastic bottles on the market today suggest many different kinds of animals. Some products come in three sizes—an ideal opportunity to create the Three Bears.

Materials

Pariscraft or papier-mâché, water, scissors, paste, paint, three different-sized bottles from the same product, newspapers.

Procedure

- Select a plastic bottle that is shaped like a bear. (Figure A)
- Crush newspaper into three balls—large, medium, and small.
- Secure these to the appropriate bottle with pariscraft

B

strips or newspaper strips dipped in paste. (Optional—If you want heavy bears, take off cap and fill with sand first.)

- Cover the bottle with smooth layers of pariscraft. Build out front paws and feet. Add a tail.
- With a stiff brush dab brown paint into the pariscraft for a fur effect. (Figure B)
- Collect many plastic bottles and save for that day when storybook animals fill the classroom.

Lesson 4   Soft Sculpture Pussycat

Objectives

Soft stuffed animals are always favorites. Welcome toys to have in the classroom, they are easy to make and fun, too.

Materials

Black sock, strong black yarn, red ribbon, yellow or white flat buttons, needle, red thread, scissors, stuffing.

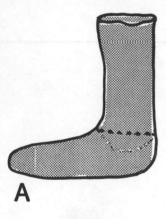

A

Procedure

- Stuff the foot of the sock with old rags, nylon stockings, or sponges.
- Pull together on dotted line as illustrated. (Figure A)
- Decide how tall you want the body and put a chalk mark to remind you. Stuff the body and tie a bright red ribbon around the neck. (Figure B)
- Chalk two diagonal lines for the ears. Sew along these lines. Stuff the head. The ears do not need stuffing. When the head is round, sew the open top of the sock with short stitches.
- With a heavy black thread gather on the diagonal lines for the ears.
- To keep the pussycat completely soft, embroider the eyes, mouth, nose, whiskers, and front paws. If yellow buttons are preferred for the eyes sew them in place. (Figure C)

B

Lesson 5   Paper Baking Cup and Oaktag Lion

Objectives

The king of the beasts is a proud jungle animal, often known for his full mane, which actually is smaller while hunting in the wilds than in captivity, where it grows to bushy proportions. The characteristics of this animal may be easily simulated using baking cups.

Materials

Four paper baking cups, 9″ x 12″ oaktag, scissors, glue (not paste), marker, crayons or paint.

Procedure

- Set aside two paper baking cups. Cut the first cup a little shorter, and the second shorter still. In this last cup draw the features in the center with a marker. (Figure A)

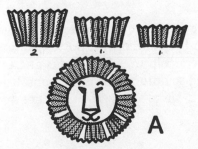

- Draw the profile of the lion's body, omitting the tail. Fold the oaktag in half and place the pattern on the fold. Cut out and stand up. (Figure B) Fold tabs for head backwards.
- Glue all the cups together beginning with the face, next larger, and finally the last two. Glue these four onto the tabs on the neck. (Figure C) Fold the last baking cup back.

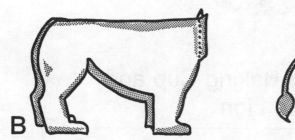

- Cut a tail and add it to the body.
- The lion is ready to stand his ground and boast his pleated mane! (Figure D)

Lesson 6   Plasticine and Toothpicks Bird

Objectives

Plasticine is a practical material for young children to handle. It can be painted with poster paints and later washed off for another sculpture. Bird walks and talks can stimulate interest in bird sculpture in this medium. Rolling plasticine in the hands is a simple way to introduce forms of different sizes.

Materials

Plasticine, toothpicks, poster paints, a branch to rest the bird on.

Procedure

- This bird can be realistic or imaginary. Shape the bird and decide on the shape and position of the wings and tail.
- Insert the toothpicks to look like a wing spread. Perhaps this is a bluejay or a cardinal with a crest on top of his head.
- Paint the bird to further identify him or color him with a gay pattern.
- Finally settle him onto a selected branch where he can watch other birds in the classroom. (Figure A) These will make unusual room decorations. A full, sturdy branch could hold several birds of all sizes, shapes, and colors.

Lesson 7 Paper Plate, Straw, and Pipe Cleaner Giraffe

Objectives

The giraffe is an unusual animal; it is often nineteen feet tall, has a distinctive pattern, no vocal cords, and can survive for a month without water. Simple materials will make a tall giraffe.

Materials

Paper plates, jumbo flex-straws, pipe cleaners, stapler, scissors, crayons or paints, box cover for display (optional).

Procedure

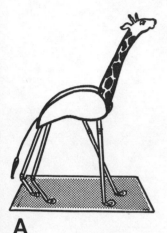

- Practice drawing the animal first. Try to get the basic proportions—the long neck, slanted body, and long legs.
- Cut the body out of the center part of the paper plates. Due to the depression in the plate there will be a three-dimensional effect when finally stapled together.
- Draw and cut the long neck and head in one piece, or cut a separate head if you prefer.
- Stuff the flex-straws with pipe cleaners, leaving a loop at the long ends for the front feet. Leave loops at the short ends for the hind feet.
- Staple a front and hind leg inside one plate. Do the same for the other plate. Now staple the two together including the neck. Add a tail.
- Paint the giraffe orange, let it dry and then paint the irregular shapes in black paint. Stand him up to eat from the trees. (Figure A)

A

Lesson 8   Life-size Pony

Objectives

Sometimes one huge project is a welcome change in the classroom, especially when it becomes a functional one. This is a community art project in which all children have a part.

Materials

Papier-mâché or pariscraft, water, paste, metal or wooden sawhorse, scrap of wood for head, scissors, newspapers, paints, string.

Procedure

- Ask the custodian to help you with the armature or frame for the horse. The metal knock-down sawhorse is good. All it needs is a piece of wood for the neck and another for the head. (Figure A)
- Crush wads of newspaper around the animal until it

A

takes the shape of a pony. Tie the paper on tightly with string. (Figure B)

- With plenty of newspaper on the floor and preferably in a corner of the classroom, begin covering with either pariscraft or papier-mâché.
- When covered, let dry and paint either a solid color or whatever pattern the class decides upon.
- In a second grade in a suburban school, one parent loaned a real pony saddle that was adjusted on the pony. The children took make-believe rides. The mane and tail were made from rope. (Figure C)

B

C

Lesson 9   Pariscraft Seal on Rock

Objectives

Seals have special appeal to small children and they are a constant joy to all who watch their expert maneuvers in the water. This is an easy shape to make and can be done successfully in almost any medium. It takes a small amount of material.

Materials

Pariscraft, sawdust and wheat paste, water, scissors, crushed newspaper, string, paints, a stone.

Procedure

- From a picture of a seal study the shape and position of its body and find a stone that will be a good resting place.
- Crush newspaper into a tight oval shape and tie it with string.
- Place strips of pariscraft dipped in water on the seal.
- Keep shaping it tightly so when it has dried there won't be soft areas.
- To hold the seal's head in an upward position, tie string to the head and tail. When dry, cut the string and the position will be as you wanted it. Keep him on the rock so the side flippers will rest flat.

- When thoroughly dry, hand paint or spray paint. Varnish or use any gloss finish for a wet look.
- The long whiskers can also be made out of thin, twisted strips of pariscraft.
- The seal is ready to jump back on the rock for display. (Figure A)

A

Lesson 10   Bas-relief Squirrel Plaque

Objectives

Working in bas-relief not only takes less material, but develops the concept of relief sculpture as well. Be sure to have plenty of research material and suggest simple ideas that pupils are familiar with. The squirrel is a good sculpture to start with.

Materials

Plasticine, cardboard, craft stick to model with, plaster of Paris (optional), soap or "Vaseline" Petroleum Jelly.

Procedure

- First cover the cardboard with a thin layer of plasticine.
- Draw the shape of the animal with a pencil.
- Roll a ball and flatten it out for the head, another for the body, and a third for the tail. The paw is shaped as a long oval.
- Begin to join these shapes and hold the plaque sideways to study the relief form.

- Add a simple landscape background or decorate with a border. (Figure A
- For an older group put the plaque in a shallow box and cover with plaster of Paris. When set, remove the plasticine; apply "Vaseline" Petroleum Jelly or soap to the inverted squirrel and pour another mixture of plaster of Paris. Let set and remove. While the mixture is setting, insert a twisted wire for a hook on which to hang the art work.

A

Bonus Ideas

Coat Hanger and Tissue Butterfly

Stretch out the hook of the coat hanger and bend the hanger to resemble wings. Cover with yellow tissue paper, gluing with waterproof glue. Design a pattern for wings with a black marker. Add a strip of black construction paper for the body.

Fantasy Animal of Rolled Newspaper

Roll newspaper into one long and two short rolls. Bend short ones over the long body form and secure with string. Crush paper for the head. Cover with pariscraft or papier-mâché.

Mexican Pottery Animal

This clay comes in a can or bag in dry form. Mix with water until clay's consistency is right for sculpture. When exposed to the air it dries slowly to harden permanently.

Monkey with Accordion Arms and Legs

Draw a profile of a monkey; paint or color with crayons. Add black-construction-paper accordion arms and legs. Tie elastic to top of head for him to spring about.

Baby Chickens

A package of cotton balls makes many baby chickens. Glue a ball onto small orange feet. Spray with yellow spray paint. With a black marker make two dots for eyes.

School Milk Carton Cat

Spray the carton any color you like. Open part of the top and glue ears in place. Use pipe cleaners for whiskers. Paint nose and eyes or glue bright buttons in place. Add a bow.

White Sock Rabbit

Stuff toe of sock with rags; tie to form tail. Fill remainder leaving enough space for head; tie string for neck and top of head. Cut end of sock to form two ears; stuff, and close. Add features.

Sawdust and Wheatpaste Birds

If sawdust is not available, shred bits of newspaper and mix with wallpaper paste to a pulp consistency. Shape birds, let dry, and paint; they will be light in weight to sit on branches or suspend in the air.

Grocery Bag Elephant

Place grocery bag on narrow end and draw wide, short legs. At open end on top draw the basic head and long trunk. Round back of elephant by crushing in the corners of the bag. This animal will be empty, just the single paper or the shape of the bag. Curve the trunk bending the end up slightly.

Cardboard Tube Animals

Cardboard tubes from paper towels form a base for an animal, either fantasy or semirealistic. Bend two inches for head, decide on length of neck. Cut other tubes for legs and tape or papier-mâché together. Add tail, ears, and other features. Spray paint.

CHAPTER 14

Proud Prints

*T*he process of transferring inked surfaces to paper is an ancient one. Today printing is a popular experience in all the grade levels. The simplest form of printing using fingers and tools can become an enjoyable lesson in the lower grades. Water-base inks and fingerpaint add to the ease of handling and cleanup. Printing can also form a good background when mixed media are involved. A collograph, for example, offers areas for brilliant color to enhance the design.

Children will be proud of their prints and can take some home and also have enough for room exhibition.

Lesson 1   Thumb Print Pussy Willows

Objectives

Children like to use their sense of touch, hence this tactile approach to printing is fun and yields effective results as well.

Materials

White tempera paint, black crayon, long panels of grey or brown paper (9" x 12" cut lengthwise).

Procedure

- Cutting the paper lengthwise is a change from the usual 9" x 12" size. It is ideal for this pussy-willow design.
- Hold the bottom of the paper and sweep a black line with the crayon; bear down hard and lift up and off

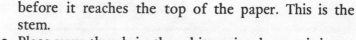

before it reaches the top of the paper. This is the stem.

- Place your thumb in the white paint, be sure it is not too thin or too thick. At the top of the branch lower the thumbnail and simply press down onto the paper just once. Figure A shows the position of the thumb.
- Dip your thumb into the paint again and begin to print the pussy willows on each side of the stem. (Figure B)
- Try to almost touch the stem. Practice on different colored papers. Let these dry, then add the shallow cup the pussy willow buds rest in. Fill this in with black crayon. (Figure C)

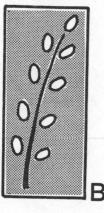

Lesson 2 Pulled Thread Prints

Objectives

This is a variation of the pulled string effect, but since the thread creates such a delicate and beautiful print it seemed wise to include it in this chapter.

Materials

Thread, magazine, poster paints, white drawing paper.

Procedure

- Practice with a 12″ length of thread first. Dip it into the color of poster paint you have selected. With the left-hand fingers, gently pull down on the thread to remove excess paint. Spiral it over a sheet of white paper letting it fall down gracefully, leaving a short piece below. (Figure A)

- Fold the other half of the sheet over it and place in the center of a magazine. Close, rest the left hand on the cover and pull the end of the thread. Press just enough to feel the thread being pulled out. (Figure B)

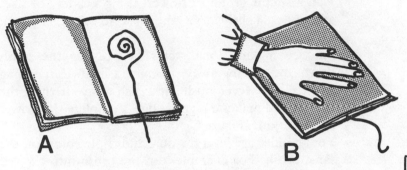

- Open the magazine and the folded paper to find a sensitive and finely lined calla lily design. (Figure C)
- These double prints can be mounted separately, cut around, and then mounted on contrasting colored paper. Or, when dry, another colored thread can be placed over the first design and again pulled. Experiment with this process to get some surprisingly beautiful results.

Lesson 3   Brush Printing

Objectives

Here is another simple form of printing in which the brush itself is the printer. It is a good way to introduce how to handle a paintbrush since they are often abused.

Materials

The #7 brush found in watercolor boxes, watercolor box, bowl of water, white drawing paper.

Procedure

- Poster paint can be used in place of the watercolors, but be sure it is thin enough. Fill the brush with color and press it down on the paper slowly. (Figure A)
- Before trying any flower printing, practice getting the right amount of color on the brush and try printing in different positions; alternate patterns including circular, clustered, etc. (Figure B)
- Plan a simple group of flowers using a variety of sizes and styles; lightly draw the basic structure in pencil first.
- Practice making long stems by pressing the brush down and pulling away, forming a light, thin ending to the line. Never push the brush away—it ruins the bristles and makes a ragged edge. Complete the flower composition. (Figure C)
- For an older age level try dual and triple colors on the same brush. For example, dip the brush into the red paint and then the green. Make a print or a long stem; the last color comes off first and blends with the second making an unusual effect. The soft blending of hues adds an Oriental mood.

Lesson 4 Potato Printing Over Blueprints

Objectives

Combine elementary science and art for a mixed media experiment. Children can easily and safely make blueprints and always take delight in watching the development of the print.

Materials

Light-sensitive paper called Ozalid, jar with wide opening and screw-on cap, small clean sponge, scissors, household lemon ammonia, scrap paper, potatoes, small piece of clear glass, masking tape to bind edge (optional).

Procedure

A

- Prepare the jar and have it ready. Place a clean, small sponge on the bottom and add a small amount of ammonia. Screw the cap on tightly.
- Always keep the light-sensitive paper well hidden between folded paper. It has a pale yellow color, this is the side to use.
- Cut shapes from scraps of paper—geometric, free-form, and images of fish, birds, etc. Practice how you plan to arrange these so you don't waste the Ozalid paper. Make the arrangement on the pale yellow side, having it near a window. Direct sunlight works quickly, so experiment on small papers first. (Figure A)
- It is ready when the yellow changes to white. Slide the pieces off, open jar and, holding the paper curved, slip it inside. (Figure B)

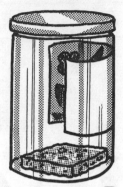

B

- Watch it develop; the design will be dark blue.
- Make several prints. A large pickle jar is ideal for classroom activity in blueprint making.
- When prints are ready and dried, plan potato printing over this soft blue tone. Use black or a dark color for contrast.
- An easy way to cut the potato is simply to cut V shapes around the edges without changing the shape of the vegetable. Using a thick potato, cut in half with one knife for a smooth surface.
- For the ink either use an ink pad, or press a finely grained sponge into fingerpaint. Then press the half potato into this pad and print over the blueprint. (Figure C)

C

Lesson 5 Collographs

Objectives

A collograph is a coined word meaning "printing a collage." It is a form of graphics used by many artists. It is a good lesson in combining textures and an excellent lesson in design judgment.

Materials

Materials, fabrics, screening, string, yarns, toothpicks, grass and leaves, scissors, scraps of paper, Duco-cement or waterproof glue, cardboard to mount materials, a brayer, water-soluble printing ink.

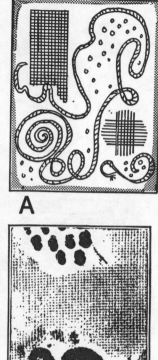

A

B

Procedure

- Practice different arrangements until one pleases you.
- Glue it on the mounting board (chipboard or oaktag are good). (Figure A)
- Let it dry thoroughly.
- Squeeze out printing ink on a Masonite board or tape waxed paper to the table and use that as your palette. With a brayer roll into the ink until it sounds tacky. Then roll over the entire design.
- Place a sheet of white paper on the collage and with the bowl of a tablespoon rub over the design carefully and evenly. Lift off and you have a collograph. Figure B shows a detail of the print showing screening, yarn, and glue dots.

Lesson 6   Three-color Monoprints

Objectives

The word "monoprint" means one print. However, many colors can be used to enrich the drawing or print and it becomes a lesson in preplanning color combinations and ink consistency.

Materials

Masonite board, fingerpaint or water-soluble printing ink, white paper, brayer, three rulers or sticks, pencil.

Procedure

- Think of a picture that will involve many lines and be balanced by solid areas. Trees along with strong shadows and bark texture make a good monoprint.

This drawing could include rolling hills, a house, and a fence. (Figure A)

- Roll the ink on the Masonite board until it sounds tacky. (Figure B) Test it first. Place a piece of scrap paper over a part of the ink and draw a few lines. Lift off—the lines should be clear. If you use too much ink no design will show.
- The first color is ready. Place the drawing face up over the ink. Arrange the three sticks one on each side and the third one across to form a bridge. (Figure C)
- Draw over the lines, shading in solid areas for the shadow on the tree or ground.
- Take off and let it dry. Plan a second color; repeat the first step, testing first. Then add a third color. Dry and mount.

A

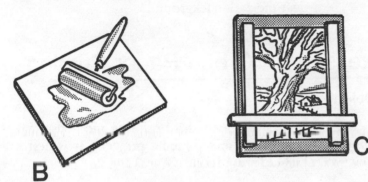

B **C**

Lesson 7   Dual Pariscraft Prints

Objectives

Although pariscraft is used primarily for sculpture, small scraps can be utilized in printing with interesting results.

Materials

Scraps of pariscraft, bowl of water, newspapers, scissors, printers' ink or fingerpaint, paper to print on.

Procedure

- Start with a simple object such as an apple. Cut it out of dry pariscraft.

A

- Spread newspaper on the work area.
- Fold a sheet of white drawing paper (or color of your choice) in half and open flat.
- Brush over one-half of the surface with fingerpaint.
- Place the pariscraft apple shape on the wet surface and fold the other half of the sheet over. Rub firmly with hands.
- Open to find two prints, one a white silhouette of an apple, and the other the pariscraft shape. (Figure A) Remove this gently. In its place will be the texture of the material.
- Let this dry, then mod podge it or paint gloss finish over it to protect the pariscraft particles from shaking off.
- The dual print can be cut in half and the white silhouette colored in with crayon—a handsome effect against the dark background.

Lesson 8   Crepe Paper Printing

Objectives

Crepe paper can be used for printing and it also makes a good background for mixed-media projects. It is best used, however, at an older age level.

Materials

Brightly colored crepe-paper folds, scissors, white drawing paper, water, sponge, newspaper for work area.

Procedure

- Fruits and vegetables are good subject matter for this process because of the simplicity of their shapes. However, more ambitious themes such as fish offer unusual results.
- Be sure your hands are dry when cutting the crepe paper.
- When the composition is ready, place a sheet of white drawing paper on the newspaper area and tape it down at the corners.

- With a sponge wet the paper but do not soak it. Gently place the cut shapes onto the wet surface. Some of the color will bleed.
- Immediately place a second paper over the first and rub with both hands. Lift off and two prints will result. (Figure A)
- One or both of the crepe-paper cutouts will remain. When dry, add a few drops of paste and secure them in place for bright accents.
- When all has dried, continue to enrich the picture with crayon or chalk keeping the second medium dry.

A

Lesson 9 Silk Screening with Paper Plates

Objectives

In this lesson silk screening can be introduced in the class on an individualized basis with each child having his own paper plate printing press.

Materials

Paper plate that is easy to cut, scissors, old curtain with fine mesh, masking tape, fingerpaint, newspapers.

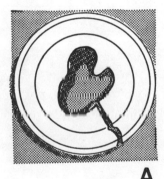

A

Procedure

- Cut into the plate from the edge, making a clean cut.
- Decide on the shape in the center. The one in Figure A is freeform.
- Cut this shape out and save it for later.
- Turn the plate over and tape the cut edge together. Stretch a piece of curtain material over the opening, securing it to the paper plate with masking tape. (Figure B)
- Turn the plate right side up and run glue around the opening to join the piece of curtain and cut edges together. Let it dry.
- On a scrap of construction paper draw around the cut-out shape. The picture must be smaller than this

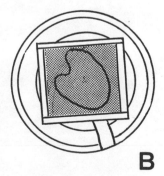

B

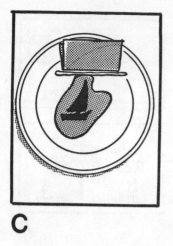

C

size. Cut out the picture and glue to the back of the opening. (See the boat in Figure C)

- Fold the cut-out shape in half. Run fingerpaint at the top of the opening and pull the folded shape down forcing the paint through the mesh. (Figure C)
- Lift the silk screen off and the print is made. (Figure D)

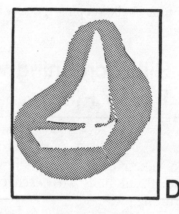

D

Lesson 10   Crushed Pariscraft Prints

Objectives

This is a good way to introduce pariscraft to those who have not yet experienced it. It only takes a small amount of pariscraft, thereby decreasing expense, classroom work area, and cleanup.

Materials

Small pieces of pariscraft, bowl of water, fingerpaint, white or colored paper (fingerpaint paper is good), flat brush, newspapers.

Procedure

- Brush a coat of fingerpaint over a sheet of paper.

- Dip a piece of pariscraft in water and crush it between your fingers.
- Holding it with the fingers, press it into the wet fingerpaint. A beautiful abstract flower form results. The plaster will collect in some areas and thin out in others giving a three-dimensional effect. (Figure A)
- Try all kinds of printing including swirling, dragging, and whatever else you can think of.
- While the background is still wet, draw stems into the flowers with the end of a paintbrush, making thin white lines that add delicacy to the picture.
- As the plaster begins to decrease, try printing on another wet fingerpaint background for a different intensity; there will be less white accents making an an even more delicate impression. (Figure B)

A

B

Bonus Ideas

Stencil Dry Brush Prints

A heavier paper such as oaktag is good; however, construction paper can be used. Cut a design leaving a one-quarter inch space between openings. Roll a ball of cotton and rub into chalk dust; dab into open spaces. Tap stencil design to shake off excess dust. These can be sprayed with pastel spray if needed.

Rubbed Crayon Prints

Cut shapes from a single theme: autumn leaves, flowers, boats, fish, etc. Place under another sheet of paper and rub with the flat side of the crayon. Hold the paper at the top and pull crayon toward you.

Finger and Fist Prints

Select fingerpaint colors and have ready on palette or in shallow dishes. Close your hand into a fist, place in paint, and print, making several in a cluster design. With a darker color dip tip of finger into paint and add centers. Try swirling the fist and dragging the fingers singly or three at a time.

Spray Prints of Found Material

Collect material on a field trip for this lesson or search in the classroom scrapbox. Arrange in an interesting composition. Spray lightly with different colors, or try a combination of gold, silver, and black.

Mixed Media and Vegetable Prints

Fingerpaint a background and print with a variety of vegetables; or print the vegetables and when dry draw a related theme around prints. Using half a small cabbage, print an all-over pattern in light grey; let dry, overlap a second printing in darker grey, and finish with a third printing of black. Dry varnish for book covers.

Plasticine Prints

Plasticine is excellent for printing since the block can be washed and reused. If clay has already been used, roll into a ball, place between two sheets of waxed paper and evenly step on it. This makes a freeform shape with a smooth surface. With a pencil make designs using both the point and the round end. Brush paint over, touching only the top surface and print.

Plaster-of-Paris Prints

Mix plaster of Paris as explained in chapter 3. Use a shallow box and fill with plaster. Carve design and spray with a varnish or fixative so the paint won't absorb. Brush paint over surface. Place a sheet of paper over it to make a print.

Tissue Printing

Colored tissue paper is good for an older group. Cut shapes of a single theme, such as sailboats, from dry tissue. Cover paper with a half-water and half-glue solution and place sail or triangle over it; rebrush with solution and the dye will yield. Lift off and reprint (it only lasts about three times). Leave the last one in place.

Gadget Printing

Collect all kinds of gadgets including bolts, cardboard tubes, small jar covers, nails, etc. Dip these in paint and print with a particular theme in mind. Plan a central design that starts with a single shape and grows outward like a snowflake.

CHAPTER 15

Jolly Games for One and All

Children delight in games. They invite anticipation, competition, relaxation, and fun. Every classroom should have on hand games of various descriptions that children can play singly, in teams, or in groups.

Many games that are inexpensive and easy to assemble can be made by the pupils. Once an idea is started, it can become a stepping stone to another creative theme.

The size and material of the games is not important, but rather the challenge in thinking that is involved. Games can include puzzles, math, spelling, colors, or just a good time in competition; all contribute to the child's world of play.

Lesson 1 Miniature Ring-toss Game

Objectives

There are many times when a quiet game for a single player is welcome in the classroom. This one is easy to make.

Materials

Permanent game: Box, sand, 1/8" dowel post, marker, pipe cleaners, and glue.

Travel or portable game: Box, round toothpicks, pipe cleaners, plasticine.

Procedure

- The portable game will be more practical for the classroom. Mark off eight places on the cover of a shallow box and number these until they total 100. (Figure A)

- Pierce a small hole at each number. Roll a small ball of plasticine and place it over each dot. Insert a round toothpick into the plasticine and hole. (Figure B)
- Twist eight pipe cleaners, using different colors, into rings. Make them into strong circles.
- The game is ready to be played. Try different distances and develop your skill with this silent ring-toss game.

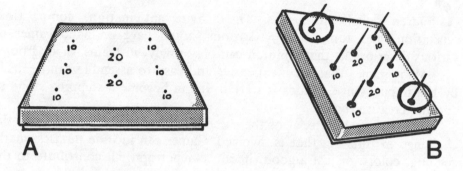

Lesson 2   Turtle Fun

Objectives

This game can include the study of turtles—their color, designs, and characteristics. It can also be a quiet pull toy.

Materials

Two paper plates, string, scissors, paints, stapler, brush.

Procedure

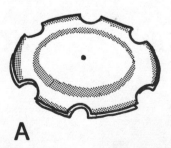

- Cut six half circles on the rims of both plates. After the first one is cut, place it over the second so the cuts line up. (Figure A) Use a 2″ diameter circle.
- Draw the head, neck, tail, and four legs out of oaktag or smooth paper. These should be about 1″ x 4″ in size. (Figure B)
- On the lower plate place the legs, head, and tail in position so they extend over the edge of the plate

about one inch. (Figure C) Punch a hole at each end and tie pieces together to a long string.

- Make a hole in the center of the top plate. Color and design the pattern of the turtle's back. (Figure D)
- Staple the top plate onto the lower in four places, pulling the string through the center hole.
- Attach a string to the part above the head to lead him.
- Take the turtle for a walk. If he's frightened just pull center string and his head, legs, and tail will disappear.

Lesson 3 "Sink 'Em" Game

Objectives

All children love to play with colorful marbles; however, marbles can become a hazard in the classroom and at home. This game has a hide-away compartment for the marbles when they are not in use.

Materials

Clean white box with lift-off cover, six marbles, long pencil, marker, masking tape, scissors.

Procedure

- Using the cover draw six circles along the sides just large enough for a marble to go through. Draw a circle at the end of the box.
- Cut out the circles and number each hole any way you want as long as it totals 100. (Figure A)
- The cover is a little wider than the base. Set this on top and with masking tape hinge the two sections together. (Figure B)
- The game needs to be set up before playing. Arrange the six marbles as in Figure A. Insert the pencil; give a push. Did you score any points? Keep trying!
- This game can be played alone or with a partner.

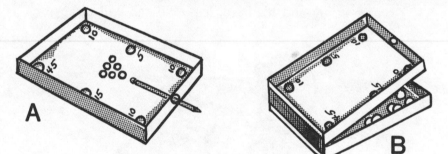

Lesson 4   Snake Jump

Objectives

Here is a hand game that can be played alone or with a classmate if each one has a snake. It is harmless and quiet, except for the squeals of delight from the players. It is a lesson in folding and cutting; design can enter into it also.

Materials

Sheet of 9" x 12" construction paper, ruler, scissors, transparent tape, piece of masking tape (optional), small box (paper baking cup box works well).

Procedure

- On the short side mark off 1½″ strips; draw lines. (Figure A)
- Cut these and fold each strip separately into eight squares.
- Tape these together to one long accordion-folded piece.
- On the last square draw a snake's head; add bright eyes. (Figure B)
- Put a sticky-side-out piece of tape on the last fold and press the folded snake into the palm of the hand. Release the fingers and let the snake jump out to surprise someone.
- When the fun is over and the snake tired out, simply put in the small box to rest. (Figure C)

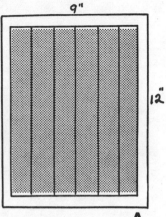

A

B

C

Lesson 5 Find the Robin's Nest

Objectives

Once this marble game is made all sorts of themes can be used. It requires little material and gives the children a chance to use their imaginations for future themes.

Materials

Shallow lift-off cover box, one marble, scraps of cardboard, scissors, paints or markers for picture.

Procedure

- Cut small pieces of cardboard and glue to each bottom corner of the box. This is to raise it slightly.
- Draw a full tree in the bottom of the box and color it.

- Draw three nests in the tree marking one *Robin.*
- Cut the three nests out just large enough for the marble to rest in it but not fall through.
- On the cover letter the title of the game. (Figure A)
- The game can be played by moving the box slowly in both hands until the marble rests in the correct nest.
- A picture of the moon could also be used. The marble will take place of the rocket and the cut-out circle will be the landing site.

Lesson 6 Egg Box Tunnel for Marbles

Objectives

The egg box is too good to throw away. It is clean and can be easily taken apart and reassembled to make tunnels for small miniature cars, marbles, and small rubber balls.

Materials

Long egg box, masking tape, tempera paints for decoration.

Procedure

- Remove all dividers and save the two ends.
- Cut two doorways in each section of the two end pieces. (Figure A)
- Close the egg box and reinsert the two ends. (Figure B)

- Spray paint or decorate with bright colors.
- There are many ways to play this game. By yourself you can put the tunnel against the wall and see how long it takes to get all the marbles inside. Or play with a partner, each having a side. If your marble goes inside your partner's tunnel you lose a turn. Create your own rules.
- Save your egg boxes—they also make good garages for your miniature cars!

Lesson 7   Land Hockey Game

Objectives

Games played with a companion need not require a great deal of space or energy. This game can be played in a moving car or at a desk in school. It can be made on a larger scale or kept small for easy storage.

Materials

Strong clean box, plastic straws, pipe cleaners, flat black button, knife, marker.

Procedure

- On each end of the box cut a long slot.
- Insert double pipe cleaners in plastic straws, leaving a twisted end protruding.
- Mark off goals at ends of the box. (Figure A)

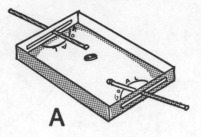

A

- Each player protects his goal with his hockey stick. If the puck enters the opponent's goal you win a certain number of points. Decide on how the scoring will be made before you begin.
- Make a larger box and get dowel posts, wrapping the ends with pariscraft. Cover a heavy object with pariscraft for the puck.
- Try original variations of this idea.

Lesson 8   Trailer Trucks

Objectives

Spools and boxes are always available. By collecting items such as these the elementary-school teacher will soon have enough so each child can have an opportunity to play with the trailers.

Materials

Boxes of different sizes, empty spools, buttons, pipe cleaners, scissors, poster paints, string.

Procedure

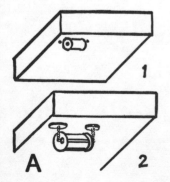

A   **1**   **2**

- Select the correct size of spools for each box.
- Measure the width of the spool and make marks wider than the spool length. (Figure A1)
- Poke two holes and insert the pipe cleaner from inside the box through a button, the spool, a second button, and into the second hole. Secure so the spool just touches the buttons. (Figure A2)
- Complete as many boxes as needed. Tie string

attaching them and add a long pull-string. The trailer trucks are ready to move! (Figure B)

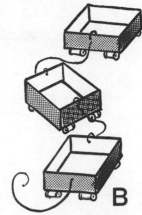

B

Lesson 9   Flying Fish

Objectives

Motion fascinates all of us and especially children. This lesson is appropriate after studying about fishes, and at the same time you can turn it into a four-player game.

Materials

Half a block of plasticine or any heavy base to support a post, knitting needle or dowel post, white drawing paper, scissors, crayons, thread, oaktag or lightweight cardboard, marker.

Procedure

- Cut two 2" x 10" cardboard strips.
- Punch a hole in the center of both of them and staple outside the holes so they form an X.
- Push the knitting needle through the hole and to prevent the X shape from slipping down make a ring of plasticine.
- Draw your fish in proportion to the width of the cross.
- Color them bright colors and mark a letter on each fish—A, B, C, and D.
- Secure the fish to the ends of each arm.
- Place a sheet of paper under the block of plasticine and mark the corners A, B, C, and D. (Figure A)
- Each player has one turn. Swing the cross once and let the fish fly around. When it stops the player whose fish stops over his letter wins.

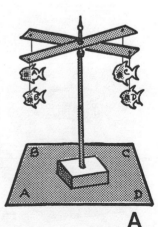

A

Lesson 10 Record Player Merry-go-round

Objective

The circus appeals to all school children and makes ideal themes for many areas including plays, drawings, cards, and games.

Materials

Record player, large record, paper plate, tissue, construction paper, paste, small ball of plasticine, scissors.

Procedure

- Use a record player with thirty-three and sixteen rpm speeds.
- Cut out your favorite comic-strip, full-length characters, animals or people, and paste on construction paper. Cut these out.
- Tape the figures to the inner circle of the record if music is to be played. Without music, place them at the outer edge.
- Roll brightly colored construction paper around a knitting needle, tape it together, and push down over the center post.
- Cut a deep fringe of brightly colored tissue paper and paste it around the edge of the plate held upside down.
- Stick plasticine one inch down from the top of the paper post and insert the paper plate carousel top.
- Turn the record player on and the merry-go-round begins to turn slowly while the fringed tissue flutters in the breeze. (Figure A)

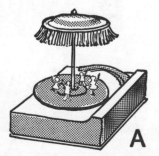

A

Bonus Ideas

Double Paper Plate Shake Game

Cut out letters or numbers. Place inside two paper plates and glue the rims together. Cut a slot at one side of the double plates on the rim for letters to be shaken out. See who finds a word first or can add the numbers that have fallen out.

Do What the Tag Says

Make tags with directions on each such as jump four times, run in a circle, hop six times on both feet, etc. Cover these with a sheet of paper and let each player take a turn.

Bowling Alley in a Box

Roll paper around a wide pencil and make paper bowling pins. Insert a small ball of plasticine half-way down inside each one to weight them. Place in a long box and bowl with a marble.

Match the Picture to the Word

Cut 4" x 5" pictures from magazines. Letter one word for each picture. Have a race to see who can match the picture to the word the fastest. Have children make their own game.

Movie Projector

Fill large cereal box with enough stones to hold it firmly. Cut an opening in the front panel and two slits at either side to thread the film through. Have each child draw a picture keeping one story in mind. Tape them together and run the movie.

Egg Box Pebble Toss

Set up egg box, marking each egg space with a number so the twelve recessed areas will total 100 points. Each player has twelve pebbles. Determine and agree on the distance to toss the pebbles from. See who gets the highest score.

Fishing Game

Peel the bark from a long, thin, straight branch and tie a thin string to the end. Adhere a small bit of masking tape, sticky side out, on the end of the string. Make different-sized fish; color, and letter the number of pounds each fish weighs on one side only. Turn fish upside down in a box and two players at a time can begin fishing. Add up the number of pounds each player catches.

Form a Three-Letter Word Race

Make up a series of letters that will make three-letter words. Lettering the words with a space apart and then cutting them into squares is easier. Turn them face down. Each player has a turn turning them over. First one to complete a word wins.

Fly a Plane into the Hangar

Make paper airplanes of different colors. Cut the base out of a bag and place on its wide side on the table or floor. Take turns for flights.

Shuffle Board Game

Design your own board with numbers. Use anything that will slide easily to represent the disk. In place of the pronged cue use a ruler or small branch that has a pronged end. Take turns.

CHAPTER 16

Galaxy of Greeting Cards

Greeting cards are a source of individual pleasure for both the giver and receiver the world over. Their messages cover a gamut of emotions, leaving a personal reaction of appreciation and warmth.

Seasonal and everyday greeting cards have a definite place in the classroom art program. Simple, folding styles are easily made in the kindergarten, increasing in complexity through the sixth grade.

A collage box collected by both teacher and pupils will be in great demand for greeting-card designing. Many of the techniques found in chapter 14 are adaptable for card making. Not only do they make an attractive wall display, but they serve a functional use as well. Everyone cherishes a greeting card made by a child.

Lesson 1   Living Christmas Cards

Objectives

Learning how to use small left-over Christmas tree branches in a functional way and creating three-dimensional fragrant cards.

Materials

Short Christmas tree branches, suitable Christmas decorations, stapler, crayons, gold or silver stars, colored construction paper, 9" x 12" white paper.

Procedure

- Fold a sheet of 9" x 12" white paper in half.
- Break branches so they measure about 6" long and spread them out on the table. Some should look like small trees and others like single branches.

A

B

- Select the tree branch and place it on the folded white paper allowing enough room for a star at the top and a container at the bottom. Staple the tree in place; decorate. (Figure A)
- Select a single stem for the candle card. Plan a short candle holder, a flame, glow, and rays. Staple in place. (Figure B)
- Select three different lengths for the landscape—a tall one near the bottom of the paper, medium-sized a little further back, and the short one in the distance. Plan the landscape—a little red house with smoke curling from the chimney spelling *Christmas*. (Figure C)
- What other ideas can you make with these fragrant branches?

C

Lesson 2   Payon on Cloth Birthday Card

Objectives

Working with Payons on a damp cloth is far more exciting than drawing on wet paper or wetting it afterward. A picture on cloth can easily be mounted to create an unusual birthday card.

Materials

Payons, bowl of water, newspapers, white drawing paper, colored construction paper for mounting, old sheeting, scissors, paste.

Procedure

- Plan designs on scrap paper first. Decide on your size and theme.
- Practice the action of Payons on wet cloth before you attempt to draw a picture or card design.
- Stretch the damp cloth on white drawing paper and tape both to the table. Draw the size in pencil and begin your greeting card design. The action of Payon on wet cloth has a brilliant result.
- Let the cloth dry while still taped so it will be flat and free of wrinkles. Trim and mount on folded construction paper of a contrasting color. (Figure A)
- Try a 12" x 18" giant greeting card of birthday wishes. Leave the name area blank. Write the child's name on a strip of paper and tape it to the card. Use over and over again.

A

Lesson 3   Pariscraft Greeting Card

Objective

Pariscraft is extremely versatile. It need not be confined to sculpture, but can make strong greeting cards, too.

Materials

Pariscraft, water, waxed paper, newspapers, scissors, paints, pencil, marker.

Procedure

- Fold a sheet of white paper in half and plan a card before using the pariscraft.
- Lay a sheet of waxed paper over plenty of newspaper.
- Cut strips of pariscraft the size needed for the card, which will eventually be a folded card.
- Dip pariscraft strips in water and smooth out over the waxed paper. This waxed paper serves two purposes: the side on the waxed paper will dry smooth and the top will have a texture to it.

A

- As the material begins to dry, divide the area of card in half by drawing a line down the center. Fold before it dries completely.
- The inside of the card will be a smooth, pleasant surface to write a message on. Design a low-relief boat on the front to make an unusual Father's Day card. (Figure A)
- Poster paints, acrylics, and markers are excellent to use on pariscraft.

Lesson 4   Crayon Etching and Mod Podge

Objectives

Crayon etching is not new, but the gloss effect created with Mod Podge is. This technique is modernized by its plasticized appearance.

Materials

Crayons, Mod Podge, white drawing paper, etching tool.

Procedure

A

- Cut the paper larger than the desired size of the finished work.
- With crayons color bands of your choice; a good range is yellow, orange, red, blue, and green. Be sure the paper is fully covered with crayon or a clear etching will not result.
- Cover these bands of bright colors with a coating of black crayon.
- By etching the top layer you will reveal the brilliant colors underneath. A simple message such as "To Mother from Byron" can burst forth in a series of colors. (Figure A)

With a flat brush dip into the jar of Mod Podge. which will be milky white in color and creamy in consistency. Brush it on in long, smooth strokes. For

a textured appearance use short diagonal strokes. Give it two coats.
- When thoroughly dry, trim and mount on bright construction paper.

Lesson 5 Pop-up Turkey Card

Objectives

Pop-up cards are easy to make once the reverse fold is understood. Try it on a larger scale first for best results.

Materials

9″ x 12″ paper, crayons, scissors, pencil.

Procedure

- Make a French fold by folding the paper into quarters.
- Place the folded edge nearest you and on the center fold mark one-third of the way down "A" to "B." (Figure A)
- Fold A to B forward and the rest of the fold backward.
- To draw the turkey, flatten the paper to an open-book fold and draw the turkey's back feathers forming a large circle. Add ground and two pumpkins for decoration and color.
- Cut the feather tips in the center fold that will finally be bent forward. (Figure B)

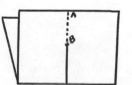

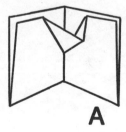

A

B

- Letter "Thanksgiving Greetings" on the cover. The pop-up turkey card is ready to surprise someone during the holiday season.
- It is fun to experiment with this type of fold—there are so many ideas that are perfect for pop-up designs.

Lesson 6   Transparent Parchment Greeting Card

Objectives

This technique is used for window transparencies. However, it also makes a delightful card that stands up featuring a see-through picture. Due to the greeting card's size it is easy for small children to handle.

Materials

Waxed paper, newspapers, colored tissue paper, leaves, grasses, threads, Elmer's Glue-All and water, scissors, construction paper.

Procedure

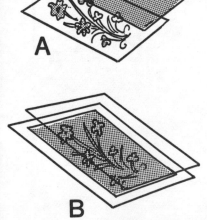

A

B

- Always plan your card first before using the materials for the finished one.
- Slide a sheet of plain paper under the waxed paper, then place this on top of the newspapers.
- Having practiced the arrangement of the materials, brush over the waxed paper with one-half glue and one-half water solution. It will resist the wax in places.
- Place the grasses and design on this wet surface.
- Cover it with a sheet of colored tissue. (Figure A)
- Brush a second coating of the glue solution over the tissue. Let it dry overnight.
- The next day place this design between two sheets of waxed paper and, using brown wrapping paper under and above, press with a hot iron. (Figure B) Peel off waxed papers.
- Trim and stand in a strip of plasticine. (Figure C)

C

Lesson 7   Blueprint Greeting Card

Objectives

The blueprint process makes excellent greeting cards. A piece of Ozalid or light-sensitive paper can be put in the ammonia jar and developed into beautiful shades of blue. A design can then be added or colored paper pasted on.

Materials

Ozalid paper, ammonia jar, scissors, colored construction paper, paste, white paint, sequins, and other decorations.

Procedure

- For the complete blueprint process see chapter 14.
- Curve a small sheet of Ozalid paper into the side of the jar and watch it develop, changing to a dark blue. Take it out before it turns completely dark and you have a beautiful background to work on. With white paint make a snow scene.
- Tracing paper is excellent to write messages on. Cut a freeform shape and write *Happy Birthday from Eunice* or a similar message. (Figure A)
- Cut flowers out of paper scraps and place at the corners. This is all done on the pale yellow side. Put it in the light near a window until the background turns

white. Immediately put it in the ammonia jar. Let it develop; take out to dry.

- Fold the construction paper into the size and shape of card you want, paste in place, and a blueprint greeting card results.

A

Lesson 8   Contac Paper Card

Objectives

A lesson without paste can be a welcome one in every grade. The numerous variations of patterns and textures in Contac paper make distinctive greeting cards.

Materials

Contac paper, scissors, construction paper, pencil.

Procedure

- Decide on the size and shape of card, single fold or French fold.
- Using a single fold, plan a frame of wood-grain, self-adhesive paper. There are many varieties. Adhere to the cover. Pull off back.
- Cut a panel of a small, bright, flower pattern and place it in the center.
- From the plain white adhesive paper cut a rabbit with a basket, making a silhouette. Put this in the center of the flowers. (Figure A)
- Think of other ideas using a wide range of textures— bricks, marble, stone, plaids, stripes, plain, wood

A

grains, flowers, and swirls. Seasonal and everyday cards are easy to make when all it takes is to cut a shape, peel off the backing, and adhere it to your card.

Lesson 9   Plastic Bag Valentine Card

Objectives

Small plastic bags give a professional look to a card. Valentine's Day is a popular time to make your own cards, and simple designs are the best.

Materials

Small plastic bags, red paper, white scrap paper, scissors, stapler, invisible tape.

Procedure

- Cut bright red paper so it will slide easily into a plastic bag.
- After you know it will fit, remove and plan your design on it.
- Hearts are popular and easy to write a message on if cut out of white paper. (Figure A)
- With invisible tape close the flap.
- Fold the card in half and slip into an envelope ready to be mailed for Valentine's Day.

Lesson 10   Miniature Finger-paint Card

Objectives

While fingerpainting in the lower grades is fun, there are times when it becomes overpowering in activity and cleanup. Why not try it on a small scale with just as much success?

Materials

Fingerpaint paper, fingerpaint, pan with water, construction paper, paste.

Procedure

- On scrap paper practice strokes and ideas that can be used for borders.
- Work directly on a Formica surface, it is easily cleaned.
- Plan to work in a 4" x 6" area.
- With the index finger start a circular border all around the rectangle. Make three of these in different colors.
- The border can be as elaborate as your design calls for. Use different-sized tools such as a toothpick for delicate lines and the end of a paintbrush for wider ones to enhance the card.
- On small bands of white paper write or letter a message such as "Get Well Soon." (Figure A)

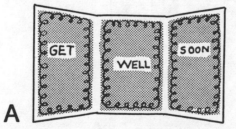

A

- Make this card in a triple fold for variation. It also stands up well. Use brightly colored construction paper to paste on.
- On the cover letter the name of the recipient and the sender.

Bonus Ideas

Rubbed Crayon Cards

Fold the card in either a single fold or a French fold. Select your theme and make cutouts that are clear in outline. Rub crayons over the front of the card and the cutouts underneath will appear.

Felt and Button Animal Cards

Using construction paper, fold a 9" x 12" sheet into quarters. Cut out an animal shape, glue on eyes with small buttons, and add a greeting.

Foil-Embossed Cards

Cut a piece of foil 1" smaller all around than the card used. Press the greeting carefully into the foil using a blunt-ended instrument. Add designs around the edge.

Stitchery Cards

On window screening outline a bird, boat, or flower. Fill it in with colorful stitchery. Staple it to a brightly colored card.

Envelope and Card in One

Use a rectangular sheet of construction paper. Plan a greeting and picture; fold the card in thirds and close with a sticker or invisible tape. Address the other side, add a stamp, and send.

Freebrush and Sequins Card

Make a French fold. Paint leaves and stems with a fairly dry brush. Paint freely, one complete stroke at a time, with no preliminary pencil work. When composition is completed add brightly colored sequins for flower centers.

Straw-Blowing Fantasy Cards

Follow the directions for straw blowing in the section "Helpful Hints and Shortcuts for Teachers." Fold and decide on the size of card. Let bright colors flow together. Add a title.

Giant Greeting Card

Use a double-page spread of newspaper. While open, draw the picture and greeting with a crayon. (A marker bleeds through to the other side.) Fold it into a rectangular shape so it will fit a business envelope. Illustrate the front with bright colors.

Accordion-Fold Card

Start with the first fold the size of a business envelope but make it one-quarter inch smaller. Tape another section on to create a longer card. Draw one large picture or make each panel a part of the story.

Wallpaper Greeting Card

Select the pattern of wallpaper in keeping with the theme, such as flowers for a birthday. Fold the card in a French fold. On the second page cut an opening so the plain side is visible for the greeting. You can also use an oval opening for the front.

CHAPTER 17

Captivating Gifts

A gift never fails to create happiness, especially when it comes from a child. Their sense of giving is genuine and direct. Parents treasure little gifts brought home from school and save them for months after the occasion has passed.

The resourceful teacher will store away a box of materials including ribbons, gift wrapping papers, yarns, sequins, and many small items that will later adorn a gift.

Lesson 1 Pencil Holder and Paperweight

Objectives

This is a good way to introduce plaster of Paris since only a small amount is needed. The material is inexpensive and makes many interesting gifts of practical use.

Materials

Plaster of Paris, water, small paper drinking cups, plastic spoon, six short pipe cleaners, newspapers, watercolors and brush or markers.

Procedure

- Spread newspaper over work area. Have plaster of Paris ready.
- Twist the pipe cleaners together in pairs so you have a set of three strong ones.

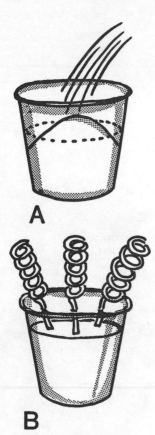

A

B

C

- Select the three pencils to be used with the gift and roll the pipe cleaners around each one, leaving a one-inch stem. Remove the pencils.
- To prepare the plaster, fill the paper cup one-half full of water and slowly sift the plaster in until a dry island forms above the water level. (Figure A)
- Stir with a plastic spoon, tapping frequently to release the air bubbles. Stir until creamy, then let it set. When it is firm enough to support the pipe cleaners, insert them in the plaster. Let them lean against the sides of the cup. (Figure B)
- Let it set. The plaster will become warm first and then cold. Pull cup away slightly from the plaster; if it makes a clean separation peel off paper cup.
- Decorate with a bright design and add pencils. Watch them wiggle! (Figure C)

Lesson 2 Plaster of Paris Swan Tray

Objectives

Here is another small gift item in which plaster of Paris is the major material. It can be made with either real clam shells or paper wings.

Materials

Plaster of Paris, water, plastic spoon, two short white pipe cleaners, small ball of plasticine, plastic ice cream dish, three clam shells or white paper for wings, jar cap for tray.

Procedure

- Prepare the head and neck by rolling a small ball of plasticine and pulling out the bill.
- Twist two pipe cleaners together and insert in the head; curve for a graceful swan's neck. Flatten the base. (Figure A)
- Prepare plaster of Paris and when it reaches a creamy consistency pour it into a plastic dish. As it sets, insert the clam shells bending and leaning them away from the head. Press the base of the neck into the plaster. Be sure the wings are in the plaster and not at the side of the dish or they will fall off when the dish is removed. Set the third clam shell in back between the wings. (Figure B)
- If clam shells are not available, make wings from white paper, studying the characteristics of these large feathers. Use the top from a small jar in place of the third shell.
- When thoroughly set, simply invert in your other hand and it will slip out, ready to decorate.

A

B

Lesson 3   Triple Tube Flower Container

Objectives

Cardboard tubes have a great deal of artistic potential, especially for gift making. This particular container can be used for dried flower or leaf arrangements or, by inserting small jars of water, real flowers can be used.

Materials

Three cardboard tubes from paper towel rolls, scissors, small jars or lumps of plasticine, poster paint or spray paint, cardboard, felt or construction paper for mat under triple vase.

Procedure

A

- Make a few sketches on paper of some ideas for different heights and placement of tubes. Also determine where you want the holes in each tube. Odd numbers always make an interesting arrangement.
- When the arrangement has been agreed upon, glue the tubes together, tying them with string to hold them until thoroughly set.
- Either paint them with colorful designs or spray paint with a single color.
- If real flowers are to be used, find small jars to place inside the tubes. (Figure A)
- If dry arrangements are to be used, fill the base of each tube with a lump of plasticine.
- Make a freeform mat for the unusual vase to stand on.

Lesson 4   "Sorry We Missed You" Door Memo

Objectives

Paper plates used singly, in multiple or cut up have a great many possibilities for interesting gifts.

Materials

Two paper plates, pencil, string, small folded paper pad, stapler, marker or paints.

Procedure

- Cut one plate in half and then shape it to resemble a hairline.
- This serves two purposes: first, it provides a place to hold the pencil; and second, it gives a three-dimensional effect. Draw in the hair.
- Staple it to the whole plate, rim to rim, so the half plate stands out.
- Lightly sketch in the eyebrows, eyes, nose, and mouth with pencil.

- Cut a sheet of typing paper into a small pad and staple together. Glue this where the nose should be.
- With a marker draw large, sad eyes with possibly one teardrop. Color in the mouth.
- On the lower rim letter "Sorry We Missed You," or use your own message.
- Lightly push a pencil through the half plate and secure a long string to it. Tie a knot at the end of the string and staple to the lower rim.
- Thumbtack the base of the plate to the door to be ready for messages when visitors find you not at home. (Figure A)

A

Lesson 5 Window Screening Placemats

Objectives

Weaving with colored yarn always delights children. Some children will work out designs, while others will experiment with color and different stitches. The finished product will serve many uses around the house.

Materials

Window screening, brightly colored yarns, scissors, crewel needle.

Procedure

- Make sketches of patterns you would like to use and study easy stitches, such as the running stitch and blanket stitch.
- Most placemats measure about 11" x 17" and dinner plates about 10".
- It is best to draw this size on paper first and sketch out your plan.
- Cut two pieces of 11" x 17" window screening and pin them together with safety pins.
- A good way to start is to make a 10" diameter circle

using a simple running stitch woven in and out of the mesh.
- Blanket-stitch the edges together as illustrated in chapter 9.
- Add other designs around the edges. (Figure A)

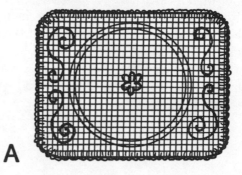

A

Lesson 6   Pariscraft Tray

Objectives

Another way to begin understanding pariscraft is to use it to cover an object. You can make a strong and useful gift by covering a shallow box cover and transforming it into a tray.

Materials

Shallow box cover, pariscraft, water, scissors, poster paints, newspapers for work area, construction paper for handle pattern, string.

Procedure

- Spread newspapers on work table. Cut up strips of pariscraft.
- Cut the handle out of construction paper and bend it over the box to determine both the height and the width. Cover it with three layers of pariscraft. While damp, place it over the sides of the box. Tie lightly with string to hold that shape.
- Cover the box's top, bottom and sides, being sure to smooth out the pariscraft and working the plaster into the mesh evenly.

- When the box has been carefully layered with pariscraft, secure the handle adding extra pariscraft so it will be strong enough for carrying and frequent handling. (Figure A)
- Decorate with simple motifs—a series of dots is always effective. Or, it can be left plain and sprayed with quick-drying enamel paint.

Lesson 7   Lazy Susan Centerpiece

Objectives

This centerpiece is the popular lazy susan. Especially fun at a birthday party, it is also a good gift that can be put to immediate use.

Materials

Pariscraft, water, scissors, two paper plates (same size or one a little smaller), knitting needle, straight branch or dowel post, paints or enamel spray, Masonite for base (optional).

Procedure

- Push the knitting needle or dowel post through the center of the plate, having the point at the top.
- Remove the plates and cover them with a smooth layer of pariscraft. Cover both sides of each plate.
- Cover the knitting needle with one layer and re-place the first plate. With narrow bands of pariscraft press firmly around the base of the needle, adhering it to the plate.
- Determine the distance between the two plates and

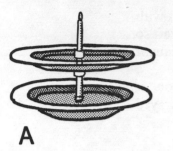

A

make a mark. Make a ring of pariscraft here so the second plate will not slip down.

- Add the second plate and again make a ring of pariscraft just above the inside of the second plate so it will turn easily.
- Create a little oval shape at the needle point. Spray paint. It is ready for use. (Figure A)

Lesson 8   Favorite Tie Rack

Objectives

Cardboard tubes are a natural material for gift making. They are thrown away daily, but if they were collected a whole class could have the fun of inventing ideas. Here is an easy one.

Materials

Cardboard tubes, wire or long pipe cleaners (a coat hanger will do), scissors or knife that can be handled safely, paints.

Procedure

- Twist long pipe cleaners together to span the length of the tube and, making a shallow triangle hanger, punch holes and secure.
- Cut out three grooves for the ties. (Figure A)
- There are many ways to cover this holder—foil, wallpaper, or plain white paper decorated with crayon or quick-drying enamel spray paint.

A

- The foil or waxed paper box itself makes a good hanger. Cut off the cover, put a strip of masking tape over the metal serrated edge, and cut slits to hang the ties on. Thumbtack the inside of the box to a door. (Figure B)
- Another method is to remove the bottom of a box, spray paint, and tack to the wall. Simply drape the ties over to make them easily accessible. (Figure C)

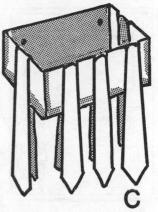

C

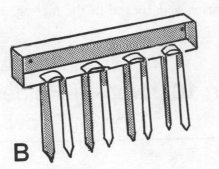

B

Lesson 9   Telephone Wall Caddy

Objectives

The telephone caddy can be designed for either a wall or table phone—the basic idea is the same. Every family will find this a welcome gift.

Materials

Cardboard for backing, colored construction paper, calendar, a plain envelope, pencil, string, pad of paper, glue, marker.

Procedure

- On scrap paper plan a design of how you want the items arranged.
- Paste a brightly colored paper on the cardboard to match the color of the room the phone is in.
- At the eraser end of the pencil, just under the metal, make a circular groove and tie string tightly around it.

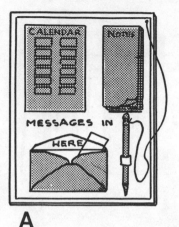

A

Use enough string for easy writing. Attach the end to the top corner of backing.

- Glue the calendar, pad of paper, and envelope to the board.
- Make a ring to hold the pencil and staple in place.
- With a brightly colored marker letter the names of each part of the caddy.
- The wall telephone caddy is ready for a message to be written and tucked in the message envelope. (Figure A)

Lesson 10   Napkin Holder
Flower Show

Objectives

A kitchen isn't complete without a napkin holder. Children find it fun to make one that is unusual and practical, too.

Materials

Two boxes about the same size, any plain plastic, two strips of plasticine, sand, glue, tape, pipe-cleaner flowers.

Procedure

- Fill the box used for the base with sand and glue the top on to prevent the sand from seeping out.
- Prepare the side panels containing the flower display.
- Either paint the backdrop a bright color or glue paper inside.
- With a knife, cut a long strip of plasticine so it fits the box. Set this inside on the bottom of the box.
- Cut short pieces of pipe cleaners and glue cut-out colored paper flowers on the ends. Insert these flowers into the plasticine. Do this on both sides of the box.
- Cover this shadow-box effect with clear plastic. Use either colored Mystik tape or regular masking tape and bind the edges.

- Glue these end boxes on the base and let set.
- This glamorous flower side show will enhance any kitchen. (Figure A)

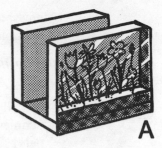

A

Bonus Ideas

Onion Bag Shoulder Pocketbook

The orange-colored onion bag has tremendous potential for art projects. Use scraps of brightly colored yarn to stitch initials on the front. Continue with border designs. Braid string and run through the top to form a drawstring; add tassels.

Crayon-Pressed Bookmarks

Cut lengths of old sheeting for width and length of bookmark. Draw designs with colored crayons and press between two layers of brown paper bag to absorb the wax. Cut edges with pinking shears.

Giant Pin Cushion

Use any plastic container similar to those margarine or cottage cheese come in. Fill a tightly woven cloth with sand and tie at the top. Invert and glue into container. Makes a huge, easy-to-use pin cushion.

Decorative Pillows with Payons

Use a small decorator's pillow that is beginning to look worn. Cut an old pillowcase to fit; add snaps or baste together when stuffed. Place brown paper underneath, wet cloth, and apply Payons in gay colors. Let dry and insert pillow.

School Milk Container Bookends

Rinse milk containers with soapy water; dry. Fill with sand and glue top shut. Use any pattern Contac paper (stone, brick, or wood grain are good). These are useful anywhere in the house and especially good for tall books.

Knitting Needle or Paintbrush Holder

Use the cardboard tubes from paper towels. Tape four together in a vertical position, stuffing each base with an inch of crushed newspaper. Glue into the base of a shallow box with as close a fit as possible. Spray paint and add a handle.

Plastic Bottle Bank

Select a plastic container of the size and shape you wish. Using an animal motif, plan the face and make a slot for the mouth. Drop pennies inside. Decorate in one of many ways. One idea is to spray paint with white and then, using a black marker, complete the animal.

Auto Food Tray

A deep box is needed for this project. Determine the number of cups needed—four is an average set. Draw around the bases of four paper cups; cut out hole and then make short slits around the circumference. This is to gently insert the cup and secure a better fit. Store paper napkins and plastic utensils inside the box with cups; it is ready for use.

Tie-Dyed Placemats

Cut strong cloth the size of placemats needed in circular, oval, or rectangular shapes. Tie-dye, dry, and iron, working from the center out. Cut colored construction paper one-half inch larger to form a border. Make a set of four for an ideal gift.

Kitchen Corner Counter Shelves

Select a strong box that is deep enough for shelves. Cut it at right angles to form a triangular shape. Use cover to make two shelves. Place lightweight objects after box is sprayed.

CHAPTER 18

Artistic Booklets

*B*ooklets of all shapes and sizes can be used in the elementary school curriculum. Many subjects require a booklet in which to record lessons, such as social studies or art appreciation. Booklets can also be used as scrapbooks for field trips or birthdays.

In the lower grades the children can learn to construct simple, single-fold books in a variety of sizes. Older groups may experiment with more complicated book construction.

The basic principles of art can be taught through booklet making. Cutting, folding, coloring, designing, sewing, and cover making all result in the creation of artistic booklets.

Lesson 1   French Fold Book

Objectives

This lesson teaches the art of folding in quarters—the French fold. The double-page format of the book prevents illustrations from showing through on the backing pages.

Materials

Lightweight paper, three sheets of typewriting paper, pencil, paints.

Procedure

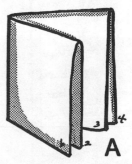

- Holding the paper vertically in front of you, fold it forward. Then fold to the right. This makes a French fold. Number the pages 1, 2, 3, and 4. (Figure A) Do this to all three sheets.

B

- On the front of the third folded sheet plan the cover's title and design.
- Staple or sew them together in the center fold. (Figure B)
- Open the cover and print small patterns over the inside end page. Here is a chance to use easy potato prints.
- Plan a theme for this small booklet: a field trip, all kinds of flowers, or characters in a story the class is reading.

Lesson 2 Envelope Snapshot Album

Objectives

The ready-made envelope, which comes in a variety of sizes, is the main material of this album. The materials are few and yet a practical folder can easily be assembled.

Materials

Six envelopes, colored construction paper, heavier colored cardboard (optional), glue, a marker.

Procedure

A

- Fold a piece of 12″ x 18″ colored construction paper in half.
- Arrange six envelopes vertically on the right-hand side after cutting off the flaps.
- Glue them on top of each other so the six pockets are facing outward.
- Press the folder thoroughly before using.
- On the cover letter "Photo Folder." (Figure A)
- A double photo album can be made by repeating the same steps on the left side allowing twelve pockets for a good assortment of photographs.
- Since this album is so easy to make, each one could contain snapshots of specific occasions such as a

special trip or a particular summer, and the cover could tell the subject matter and the dates. These could then be filed for an impromptu showing.

Lesson 3 Revolving Circular Book

Objectives

Revolving folders are fun and not that hard to make. With a few envelopes, a pencil, pipe cleaners, and a lump of plasticine, a new look to booklets results.

Materials

Four envelopes or as many as you like, a long pencil, pipe cleaners, lump of plasticine, paper puncher.

Procedure

- Fold the flap of each envelope back and then fold the envelope in half so the flaps are touching.
- Mark four holes and punch through one-quarter inch from the fold. Place the punched-hole folded envelope over the others and mark where the holes will be. Punch the other envelopes.
- Cut 6" pipe cleaners in half and thread through the holes of the folded envelopes, joining as smoothly as possible.
- Form a mound of plasticine and press it firmly on a small piece of cardboard.
- Insert the long pencil through the pipe cleaner rings and press onto the plasticine. (Figure A)
- The circular book is ready to be revolved to display snapshots, special clippings, or postcards.

A

Lesson 4 "Growing Page" Birthday Book

Objectives

A birthday is a special occasion to every child. Here is a way to celebrate the day with a classroom "growing page" birthday book. The birthday cake inside can be elaborately colored, but make a cut-out one that can be retaped for another card.

Materials

18" x 24" pastel colored construction paper, 18" x 24" white paper, 9" x 12" white paper, masking tape, marker, colored crayons.

Procedure

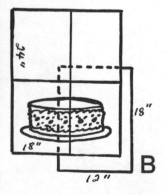

- Fold the 18" x 24" pastel colored paper into quarters so it opens like a book.
- Fold the 18" x 24" white paper in half the wide way.
- Paste the folded colored paper in the center on the right-hand side of the folded white paper. (Figure A)
- On the cover letter *"Watch Your Birthday Grow."*
- Let the birthday child open the book. (Figure B) On the big sheet will be a 10" wide birthday cake beautifully decorated. Let him draw in his birthday candles and write his name under the cake.
- The teacher can make a birthday-cake cutout and this can be adhered with masking tape, sticky side out, so the cake can be used over and over. Of course the child may want to take it home, so have a pattern ready!

Lesson 5 Tall Bag Storybook

Objectives

Here is another chance to use the versatile brown paper lunch bag. It makes an excellent original storybook. The child could insert his story in the right-hand flap and paste his picture of the story on the left side.

Materials

Two brown lunch bags, white paper for picture and lined paper to write the story, crayons, marker, stapler.

Procedure

- Hold the bag with the flap side up.
- Mark off a frame just above the flap on the first bag.
- Cut drawing paper so it will just fit inside the frame.
- Write the story, fold it in half, and insert in the flap of the second bag.
- Illustrate the story in bright colors and paste in the frame.
- Staple the two bags together to make a binding.
- On the cover letter the name of the story and the name of the artist. Adding the date would be a good idea, too.
- Now open the tall bag book, enjoy the picture, and read the original story. (Figure A)

A

Lesson 6 Magazine Book

Objectives

The small 8½″ x 11″ magazine is ideal for this book. What results is a tall, narrow book, full of blank pages for drawings or clippings.

Materials

Small magazine (8½" x 11"), typing paper, construction paper, paste, markers or crayons.

Procedure

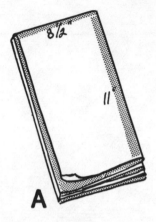

- The average small magazine has about 226 pages in it. This book only needs about one-fourth of the magazine. Tear the magazine off at page fifty-six. One magazine will yield four tall books.
- Fold each magazine page in half folding toward you. Do this to all the pages. You now have twenty-eight pages. (Figure A)
- Fold twenty-eight sheets of typing paper in half the long way and slide each one over each magazine page. (Figure B)
- Do this to all the pages, pasting them at the four corners of the typing paper sheets.
- If the magazine pages are folded over so they tuck into the binding, they will be secure enough not to slip out.
- With colored construction paper make a cover and glue the first and last pages down. Press the whole book before using it.
- These tall blank pages are fun to draw on or paste clippings.

Lesson 7   Roll-around Picture Book

Objectives

For a novel change of format the children may like to make the roll-around picture book. Instead of turning pages, the story is presented by a series of small pictures on a revolving cylinder.

Materials

Coat hanger, cardboard tube, scissors, masking tape, one sheet of 18" x 24" white or colored paper, paste.

Procedure

- It is easier to cut the cardboard tube to insert the coat hanger than to untwist the top of the hanger and separate it.
- Slide the tube around the wire, tape together again and bend the ends of the hanger upward to keep tube in place. (Figure A)
- Cut the white 18" x 24" paper vertically to make two 24" x 9" strips. (Figure B)
- Tape together to make one long strip. Leave it flat to paste pictures on later.
- Plan a 5" x 7" drawing. This may either be a collection of pictures from the whole class on one topic or pictures collected during the month—excellent for P.T.A. night.
- When the pictures are ready, paste them on, leaving a white border around each picture.
- Place around the tube and tape. The story unfolds as you roll the picture book around! (Figure C)

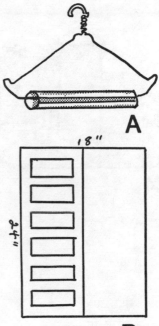

Lesson 8   Farm Book

Objectives

While studying a particular unit such as the farm, a related project in the form of a book would be appealing to the children. While this project may involve the use of a pattern, which is not a favorable way to draw, it could be the child's own drawing of the farm that becomes the actual shape.

Materials

12" x 18" construction paper for the cover, white drawing paper, crayons, paints, stapler.

Procedure

- Draw around the pattern first using the construction paper and then begin the story of the farm on the white drawing paper. Staple for binding.

- The book could contain the work of the whole class illustrating animals, foods, shelter, products, farm trucks, helpers, etc. This is another way to make a concentrated collection of the work of the total class—a good idea for P.T.A. night.
- Title the book *The Farm*. (Figure A)

A

Lesson 9   Lace Doily Book

Objectives

For an unusual and delicate book that is totally different use lace doilies.

Materials

Eight lace doilies (5" diameter, round), pink ribbon, paper, marker, stapler, small clippings from magazines or pictures drawn by the children.

Procedure

- While this lace doily booklet is extremely simple, it has a delicate air to it and can be used with a variety of illustrations including small cut-out snapshot portraits, flowers cut from magazines, flowers drawn by the children, or favorite scenes.
- Two lace doilies form the covers. Letter a title for the cover; a marker works well for this.
- Since there are six pages, twelve pictures are needed to fill the book. Paste on both sides of each doily.
- Add another bit of color on the cover with a circle of pastel colored paper pasted in the center—a 2" diameter is fine. When all the pictures and pages are ready, staple them together and add a bright bow. (Figure A)

A

Lesson 10 See-through Paper Plate Book

Objectives

Thin paper plates make a compact book since each plate is inside the other. There is always a supply of clear plastic to use, including plastic bags from the cleaners. The pictures in this book should be of a single theme.

Materials

As many paper plates as needed (two plates to a page), plastic sheeting, masking tape, stapler, cutouts. A ring works well for the binding.

Procedure

- Cut directly in from the edge to the center and cut out a circle, square, or freeform shape.
- Cut plastic or use cut-up plastic bags to cover the opening.
- Tape the corners down with masking tape, smoothing out the plastic to make it free from wrinkles. (Figure A)
- Use the cut-out shape as a pattern and cut the second plate to match the first one. Tape the cut edge on both plates and staple.
- Decide on the subject matter for the see-through opening. It can be made from colored tissue paper, silhouettes, or whatever you like. Glue this in place.
- Staple the second plate over the first and this page is ready.
- Make three pages and punch a hole for the ring. (Figure B)

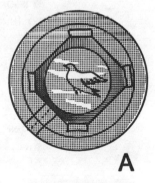

A

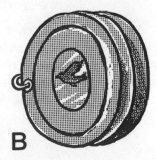

B

Bonus Ideas

Pop-Up Books

Refer to chapter 16, lesson 5 for instructions for a pop-up card. Decide on your theme and tape the pages together for an amusing pop-up book.

Match Folder Score Booklet

Remove the few remaining matches or save empty match folders. Cut typing paper the length of an opened folder. Staple enough pages together for easy closing. Add a small piece of Contac paper for cover to hide advertising. You have a handy pocket score booklet or memo pad.

Envelope Folder, Loose Pages

Using long business envelopes, staple at the fold's top, middle, and bottom. Add a cardboard cover taping pages to center back. Either cut off flaps or close envelopes. Personalize cover with initials.

Oriental Style Accordion-Fold Book

Fold several sections in accordion style. Decide on number of pages needed. Make a cardboard cover, scoring the cardboard with end of scissors down the center. Glue front page to front cover, back page to back cover. This book can stand with the center pages springing out.

Spiral Book

Fold colored construction paper in half making 6" x 9" double vertical pages. Punch three holes on each folded page. Assemble all pages and make pipe-cleaner rings through each hole. Six colored sheets make a twelve-page book. You have one page for each month of the year or a memo book.

Large Newspaper Scrapbook

Open a double-page newspaper and fold horizontally, lightly pasting edges so two wide pages of double newspaper results. Add more until you have the size needed. Make a plain cover and secure pages with large brass fasteners for appearance as well as functional use. Paste bright, sharp-colored pictures of all kinds of trucks, airplanes, and missiles, for a Transportation Scrapbook.

Scroll Books

Hold 12" x 18" white paper horizontally. Find two straight, smooth sticks or branches and glue to each 12" end, winding around just to cover stick. Plan story or pictures inside. Roll up and add brightly colored ribbon, which can be attached to the center back.

Plastic Baggie Books for Nature Studies

Collect Baggies that have the folding top. From nature walks save leaves, flowers, bark, etc. Staple these through the Baggie. Make a cover and staple all pages together. Make new ones for new walks.

Coat Hanger Flip-Over Books

Staple sheets together around the base of a coat hanger. Make a fold line for easy flip over. Use five sheets for the best papers of each day. Let children flip them over for new accomplishments.

First School Day Class Book

Use 9" x 12" brightly colored construction paper. Paste two smiling faces on the cover—a little boy and a little girl. Staple a few pages together for children to write their names. This makes a nice memento for the end of the year, or added item for classroom visits during P.T.A. night.

CHAPTER 19

Pageant of Decorative Papers

*B*right, gay, decorative papers can develop through accidental, experimental, and preplanned designs. Decorative papers can be used for gift wrappings, background mounts, lettering, cutouts, collage pictures, end pages in handmade books, and mixed-media lessons.

Plan this activity with plenty of space and materials so the children can explore the making of decorative papers.

Lesson 1   Marbleized Paper

Objective

This historical paper was a secret craft developed during the sixteenth and seventeenth centuries. It consisted of intricate and delicate swirling designs obtained by stirring floating oil colors on water. The bookbinders of England used these beautiful and decorative papers for the end pages of books.

Materials

Artists' oil colors (not house paint), low shallow pan, foil, newspapers, stick for stirring, water, white paper smaller than the pan.

Procedure

- Spread newspapers over the work area.
- Any colors can be used, but white, black, red, blue, and yellow are excellent for unusual results.
- Mix each color separately in a small can with turpentine to a thin, creamy consistency.

- Fill pan half full of water. Drip in the colors.
- Stir slowly until a design or pattern pleases you. (Figure A)
- Hold the white paper in both hands and curve it, bending the sides up over the water. (Figure B)
- Let the curved part touch the water first then the sides until it is flat on the water. Lift it up by one corner and set aside to dry. You can restir this many times before adding more color.

Lesson 2   Antiqued Paper

Objectives

Exploring color combinations and crushing paper can result in a paper that resembles very old paper. As the paper surface is crushed it cracks, allowing the watercolor to absorb forming thin and ragged lines all over the paper. When dried and smoothed by ironing, a handsome paper is ready to use.

Materials

White drawing paper, watercolors, water, sponge (optional), iron.

Procedure

- Watercolors or poster paints can be used.
- Spread newspaper on the table and place the white paper in the center. Sponge the whole surface with water.

- With a brush paint patches of colors over the area: yellow, orange, green, red, blue, and violet. (Figure A)
- When all the paper has been covered with color, pick it up and simply crush it together firmly in both hands. (Figure B)
- Open it and smooth it out. When dry, put brown paper on the ironing board for protection and iron it flat. A textured pattern develops, which is original and colorful. It can be used to draw and paint on, for cutouts, or as a frame for drawings. It also makes striking gift wrapping paper.

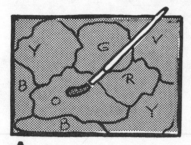

A

B

Lesson 3   Brayer Rubbings

Objectives

While crayon rubbings are fun, brayer rubbings are full of surprises. They give the exact picture and not a reversed one as in block printing.

Materials

Brayer; water-soluble ink (or fingerpaint); scraps of paper, leaves, string, screening, etc.; glue; cardboard; newspapers; Masonite or waxed paper to roll ink on.

Procedure

- Prepare the work area with newspapers.
- Spend several minutes arranging the materials to form a good design.

- When one has been decided on, glue materials in place on a cardboard backing.
- Squeeze some ink onto a Masonite board or a sheet of waxed paper taped to the table for a palette.
- Roll the brayer into the ink until it sounds tacky.
- Place a sheet of drawing paper over the design and tape it at the corners.
- Roll the brayer evenly over the entire surface. The design underneath will be seen in a darker tone. (Figure A)
- More colors can be added and the brayer rolled over only part of the print. Any variety of ways of applying color can be experimented with.
- Use a sheet of newspaper and make a repeat design on the financial section where no pictures are used.

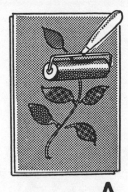

A

Lesson 4 Waterproof Ink and Wet Paper

Objectives

Although not a great deal of skill is required in this paper design, there are times when accidental effects are fun to watch. When waterproof ink is combined with water on paper, an action takes place that resembles the burst of a skyrocket into infinite particles. It would be almost impossible to describe these patterns with words.

Materials

White drawing paper, black waterproof ink, newspapers, #7 brush, water, sponge.

Procedure

- With newspaper in place set up a bowl of water and sponge.
- Sponge clear water over the drawing paper, so it is really wet. (Figure A)
- Dip the brush into the black ink, have it full but not dripping, and, holding it at a sharp slant, touch the

paper with the tip of the brush. (Figure B) Immediately a black circle will appear, spreading into a delicate fringe around the circle.

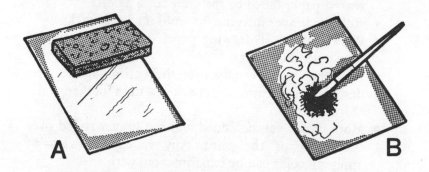

- Add another touch of the black ink and watch it crawl over the wet surface. If part of the paper begins to dry, simply sprinkle a few drops of water on the paper and continue to enhance the pattern of accidental designs.
- When this paper has dried, it can be used for unlimited ideas. It will not rub off and will invite many questions as to how it was done.

Lesson 5   Watercolor Wet Method

Objectives

Often a delicate pastel paper is needed as a background in mounting or packaging. In addition to serving these needs, this lesson can also be used to watch two colors run together to make a third one.

Materials

Watercolors (considerably thinned poster paints can also be used), sponge, water, white paper, brush.

Procedure

- Set up the work area. Open watercolor box, wet the colors, and let them absorb the water for a few minutes.

- In beginning this experiment, use only the primary colors at first: yellow, red, and blue.
- In the watercolor box cover place a puddle of water and roll off yellow; test this color for strength on a piece of white scrap paper. Add another puddle, and do the same with blue. Make another one red.
- Place the white paper in front of you with newspaper under it and start with a large yellow patch in the upper left corner; rinse the brush and add a blue patch in the upper right corner; watch the two colors overlap to make green. (Figure A)
- After you have tried the three primary colors you will find that orange, green, and violet have been made. Now try other colors to see what happens when they run together.
- Let the paper dry and use for block printing, end pages, gift wrapping, or greeting cards.

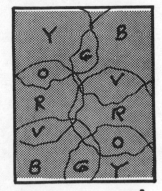

A

Lesson 6 Waxed Paper and Watercolor Resist

Objectives

Waxed paper is inexpensive material for the classroom and yields interesting effects. It is also adaptable to various techniques.

Materials

Waxed paper, watercolors, #7 brush, a tool with a blunt end, white wax crayon, white drawing paper, newspapers, water.

Procedure

- Prepare work area. Have your materials within easy reach.
- Open watercolor box and pour a puddle of water into one of the sections. A darker color such as blue is better than a light one. Test to be sure it is strong

enough by making a brush stroke on a piece of scrap paper.

- Place a sheet of waxed paper over the sheet of white drawing paper.
- Repeat lettering over the paper. Make sure the letters are big and wide. Rub with the blunt tool over the letters, which can be done freehand. This step transfers the wax to the white drawing paper.
- With a good sized brush paint over the white paper beginning at the top, go straight across, repeat this all down the paper. Watch the watercolor resist the wax and leave small particles on the wax area. Try a white crayon for a similar effect. (Figure A)

A

Lesson 7 Crumpled Newspaper and Enamel Spray

Objectives

This activity is good for older children who have already used spray paint and like something new that has surprising results. It is a good way to teach them how to use spray paint correctly and how to protect both themselves and classroom furniture.

Materials

Small cans of spray paint, newspaper, white and colored paper, plastic Baggies, box for spray booth, apron.

Procedure

- Place the box (spray booth) in a well-ventilated corner of the room.
- Plan to have old shirt or plastic aprons, which are best, for protection.
- Crush a single sheet of newspaper into a ball and place in the booth.
- Use a Baggie to cover the hands to protect them from the spray and spray the crushed ball of paper. (Figure A)

- The ball of paper can be pushed around with a stick and another color, or even three colors, can be sprayed.
- When thoroughly dry smooth out. Paper can be dampened on the back with a sponge to flatten it.
- Try crushing a brightly colored large magazine page and follow the same procedure. Open to find sprayed irregular shapes over areas of bright color. The picture is not a recognizable object, which is the desired result. The spray takes on a glossy appearance.

Lesson 8   Crayon Batik Paper

Objectives

If the art of batik making has been studied, this is a good and easy follow-up lesson. Crayons and watercolors provide an introduction to this ancient art.

Materials

Crayons, watercolors, white drawing paper.

Procedure

A

- In this lesson, think in terms of design rather than a realistic drawing. Select easy themes such as flowers, boats, fish, or fruits.
- Draw these lightly in pencil first and then heavily with crayon making a strong coat of wax over the design. Leave the background white paper.
- Mix a large puddle of watercolor with a strong color and test on white scrap paper first.
- Paint over the entire paper with a bright wash, going over the heavily waxed crayon. Little particles of paint will stay on the wax, but most of it will resist. Color will collect in small puddles which is good as it lends a three-dimensional look to the design. (Figure A) The paper is then held up for the watercolor to run down a little.
- This paper can also be crushed enough to crack the wax crayon area and for the watercolor to creep in for a crackled effect.

Lesson 9   Wash-away Technique

Objectives

Poster paint and waterproof ink form another technique that requires practice to get the most out of the process. Black and white designs are just as attractive as the ones in bright colors.

Materials

Poster paints, black waterproof ink, brush, a sink in the classroom.

Procedure

- Poster paints are used full strength in this technique.
- There are two ways of doing this, either having a black background or colorful one. For the first attempt the solid black area is better.

- Paint bold designs leaving narrow lines of white paper between the colors. This will prevent them from running together.
- Let it dry thoroughly. Then cover with one coating of the black ink.
- Turn the faucet on to a moderate stream of water. Hold the art work flatly under it and let the water break away the top layer of ink revealing the brilliant colors underneath. The background will absorb the ink; it will only flake away where there is a layer of poster paint under it. Pull the paper away from the water so all the ink is not washed off. Particles of ink should remain. Three steps are shown in Figure A.

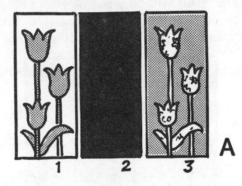

Lesson 10   Crayon and Mod Podge

Objectives

There is nothing more refreshing than a shiny paper—it has a clean and pleasant-to-touch surface. A lesson in repeat designs with the ordinary crayon can be glamorized by this finishing touch.

Materials

White drawing paper, crayons, Mod Podge. (Scraps of broken crayons can be used, too.)

Procedure

- 9" x 12" white paper is good to start with. Discuss design by looking for it in the classroom, especially on childrens' clothes. Notice how a simple design or shape, when repeated in an orderly fashion, can be gay and pleasant to look at.
- When the pattern has been finished, pour some Mod Podge into a clean dish. Use a flat brush and, with long strokes, paint over the entire designed paper with this solution. It will look like milk and be opaque at first. After the first coat begins to dry it will turn transparent. Two coats can be used; paint in the opposite direction the second time.
- The result will be a plastic-effect finish on the child's decorative paper, ideal for gift wrapping, booklet covers, greeting cards, etc. (Figure A)

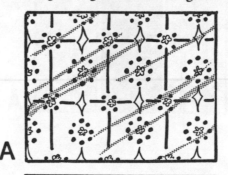

Bonus Ideas

Straw-Blowing Designs

Refer to the section "Helpful Hints and Shortcuts for Teachers." Straw blowing results in accidental spidery patterns that, when mixed with other colors, creates unusual effects for numerous purposes.

Vegetable Printed Patterns

Using a vegetable create simple, all-over, repetitive designs to more complicated shading arrangements. Depending on their use, these can be spray varnished, shellacked, or left plain.

Drip Painting Papers

Brown wrapping paper or cut-open grocery bags make a strong

material for wrapping gifts or book covers. Drip paint from a brush, but not in blobs; just let it drip moving the brush constantly. Also, hold paper at an angle for further running of colors.

Fingerpaint and Comb

Spread fingerpaint over the surface of fingerpaint paper and, using a variety of sizes of combs, make swirling, curved, and straight lines. Keep strokes clean so lines are visible patterns.

Spray-Painted Papers

Use cutouts or found objects of a single, appropriate theme: leaves for autumn ideas, flowers for spring, and so on. Place on white, colored, or brown paper and spray with a paint gun, quick-drying enamel, or use the toothbrush and screen method. For the latter, dip an old toothbrush in poster paint and pull it across a small piece of window screen. This will cause a spattered effect as the paint is forced through the mesh.

Crayon Etching Paper for Small Gifts

Cover paper with brightly colored crayon patches, ending with a black layer. Etch through any designs you wish.

Dry-Brush Technique Papers

Dip small house brush in paint and drag off excess paint on newspaper. Pull strokes toward you leaving a multiple of fine lines. Experiment with vertical, curved, latticed, and overlapping strokes for unusual results. Keep all black or combine colors.

Newspaper Tie-Dyed Papers

Since newspaper tears easily this has to be done with the least possible handling; however, the results are interesting. Tie the newspaper gently, dip in bright dye, let dry, cut string, and iron.

Tin Can Rolled-String Papers

Use long tin cans or a rolling pin; paste or glue shapes, including string, to it with a waterproof solution. Brush paint on and roll over paper in one direction or in an overlapping pattern.

Cut-Flower Sponge Papers

Cut petals from sponges and print freeform designs all over the paper in a galaxy of blossoms. Use pastel colors; a garden variety of flowers will result so paper can be held in any position.

CHAPTER 20

Merry Mobiles, Stabiles, and Kinetics

Mobiles, stabiles, and kinetics are fascinating forms of sculpture in contemporary art. The ever-moving mobiles, the stationary stabiles, and the combination of both, kinetics, offer endless creative art projects for all ages.

These three art forms have a strong appeal to children—they can try their skill in balancing, constructing, and designing three-dimensional art. As art lessons they have many advantages: they require small space, team work, inventiveness, and use of accessible materials. They also provide successful lessons for children less talented in drawing and painting and, conversely, they widen the talents of the more artistic child.

Lesson 1   Mobile—Paper Strip

Objectives

This is one of the easiest ways to make an attractive mobile from strips of colored paper. All sorts of color combinations and shapes can be explored with just five strips.

Materials

Strips of colored construction paper or Dubl-Hue paper, thread, paper clips, scissors, stapler, paper puncher.

Procedure

- Cut strips from 9" x 12" paper about one inch wide. Plan a center color and repeat the color combinations on each side.

- Staple the five strips together at the top.
- Hold the center strip straight and push the two on the left side up and out forming curves of two depths. (Figure A) Staple.
- Repeat on the other side and staple in place so each side balances.
- Curl the ends inside.
- Either cut off the center strip, fringe it, or curl it any way you wish.
- Make others, changing the design and the colors.
- Plan the basic mobile frame and secure the strips in place. (Figure B)

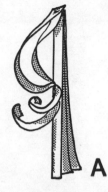

A

B

Lesson 2   Mobile—Color Wheel

Objectives

This color mobile can be made in a variety of media: crayon, watercolor, parchment, etc. It is a good way to explain the results of color mixing and serves as a reminder of the color wheel.

Materials

Crayons, watercolor, or whatever the desired medium; threads; mobile frame to hang parts on (coat hanger, wire, etc.); scissors; paper puncher.

Procedure

- Cut seven colors in different shapes; pleasing abstract shapes are good.
- Punch holes at the top of each one and tie threads to them.
- Stretch a coat hanger as wide as possible and turn the ends up.
- Plan the shape with letters for each color so they are arranged as in Figure A.

A

- The hanging shapes will illustrate how two colors mix to create another color: blue and red make violet; red and yellow make orange; and yellow and blue make green.
- A hanging mobile will turn in the air and act as a reminder of the color wheel in an interesting manner.

Lesson 3   Mobile—Parchment

Objectives

Transparent decorative art paper is ideal for mobiles. It is easy to cut and shape, has unusual color harmonies, resembles stained glass, and will attract admiration in the classroom.

Materials

Colored cellophane drinking straws, threads, pipe cleaners. Chapter 16, lesson 6 covers the process of making parchment, including materials.

Procedure

- Follow the procedure for making parchment paper discussed in chapter 16.
- Place the drinking straws on the table and decide on a plan for the general design of the total mobile.
- For added strength punch pipe cleaners through the straws. This also makes the joining of two straws firm.
- The mobile can include many parts of various shapes or it can be of one theme such as a fish. (Figure A)

A

- Draw the fish on a paper first and then place the pipe cleaners over the pattern. Shape and join to make a fish outline.
- Plan elongated scales or any interior design you wish. Cut these out of brilliantly colored parchment paper. Punch holes and tie the shapes to the top of the fish. Watch it move in the air current.

Lesson 4 Mobile—Cardboard and Thread

Objectives

This experiment in color is exciting as the use of overlapping threads increase and lessen the intensity. It is a freeform lesson allowing pure, abstract, individual expression.

Materials

Spools of thread in bright colors, pieces of various colored cardboard in abstract shapes, scissors, coat hanger for frame, paper puncher.

Procedure

- The cardboards can be precut and pupils can select the ones they prefer.
- Discuss color and take one shape, cut out the center, and begin to experiment.
- Cut two slits on the right side. On the opposite side cut ten slits.

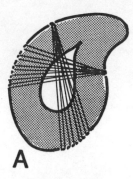

- Begin with knotted thread and secure in a right-hand slit. Carry thread over the front to the first slit on the other side and into the second slit, around the back and into the first slit on the right again. Repeat this until all the ten cuts on the left have been filled. With a little glue or knot end the thread. (Figure A)
- Cut two slits at the top and eight at the bottom and repeat the process. Make others and hang the mobile. (Figure B)

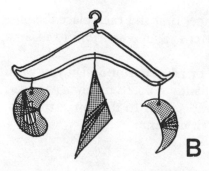

Lesson 5 Stabile—Tissue Paper and Pipe Cleaners

Objectives

This lesson increases awareness of the importance of space, an essential factor in designing stabiles. Tissue paper, because of its transparency, is perfect for this stabile.

Materials

Colored tissue papers, pipe cleaners, waterproof glue, block for platform, scissors, waxed paper.

Procedure

- Plan your idea on scrap paper first and change if necessary as you go along.
- Form a shape out of pipe cleaners, twist together and form a stem.
- Place it on waxed paper to prevent sticking.

- Run a line of glue on top of the pipe cleaner. Place a sheet of colored tissue paper on top of the waterproof glue. (Water-soluble glue will make the tissue-paper color run.) (Figure A)
- Make an odd number of shapes and vary them in size for a more interesting composition.
- When these shapes have dried, place them in a block of plasticine and arrange so the stabile has as pleasing space shapes as the tissue forms. (Figure B)

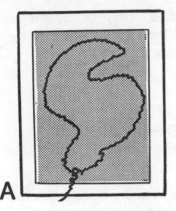

A   B

Lesson 6   Stabile—Toothpicks and Cellophane

Objectives

All children like to work with toothpicks. They can invent all kinds of forms with them.

Materials

Boxes of flat toothpicks, glue, pieces of colored cellophane, base (plasticine is good), flat craft sticks for the stems, waxed paper.

Procedure

- Always plan ideas on scrap paper first. To make individual parts to this stabile, arrange the toothpicks in different designs, slightly breaking them for bent

positions and keeping them straight for radial sunbursts and other patterns.

- Place a sheet of waxed paper over the designs and follow them by placing the toothpicks in place, gluing them as you go along. (Figure A)
- When these have set thoroughly, lift them up and think out a space relationship in unified grouping.
- Cut the plasticine base in a square or circular shape and insert the forms. Glue cut pieces of colored cellophane to the parts at different angles. (Figure B)
- If spray paint is desired, spray before the colored cellophane is added. Glue a piece of felt on the base so the oil will not mar the furniture.

A

Lesson 7 Stabile—Pariscraft

Objectives

Pariscraft is also good for stabiles since it dries strong, shapes easily, and can be sprayed or painted by hand.

Materials

Pariscraft, water, scissors, newspapers, waxed paper, brick or block of wood, scraps of black paper, glue, paints.

Procedure

- Music is the theme of this stabile.
- Spread newspaper over the work area and place a sheet of waxed paper over it.
- Cut strips of pariscraft and dip in water. Smooth out on the waxed paper. Three coats are fine.
- As it begins to dry, pick it up and spiral into a cone shape. Make three using different sizes.
- Arrange the cones on the base that has also been covered with pariscraft. To hold the spirals at an angle, merely crush balls of newspaper and let cones rest on them. Secure these to the base with pariscraft.
- Cut out black notes and arrange in interesting manner. (Figure A)

B

Lesson 8   Kinetic—Flat Papier-mâché

Objectives

Kinetics combine both mobile and stabile because some parts move while others are stationary. More advanced kinetics will continue to move for a long time if motion is started; however, this requires a good deal of skill. The elementary school child can explore this form of sculpture in a simple manner.

Materials

Coat hanger, thread scraps of paper, rock or lump of plasticine, tape, newspapers, wallpaper paste for the flat papier-mâché, scissors.

Procedure

- Select a lightweight coat hanger that is easy to bend.
- Shape it into a stylized body and wings of a bird. (Figure A)
- Draw a pattern for neck and head of the bird.
- For the head layer three pieces of newspaper together with wallpaper paste in between. Smooth out wrinkles and cut out head.
- With short strips of newspaper paste the flat papier-mâché head and neck to the coat-hanger frame.
- From the left-over pasted newspaper scraps shape a long worm.

- Tie a thread to the end of the worm and secure to the bill of the bird so it will move with the air currents.
- Tape the coat-hanger hook to a rock or lump of plasticine. The stabile and mobile combination make a simple kinetic. (Figure B)

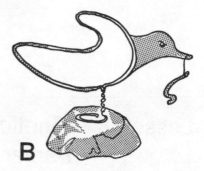

B

Lesson 9   Kinetic—Four Seasons

Objectives

In this simple, balanced kinetic, using the four seasons symbols is an opportunity to try balancing different sizes of paper through experimentation until an equal balance is established.

Materials

Straws, pipe cleaners, construction paper, scissors, threads, paste.

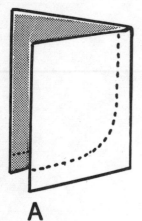

A

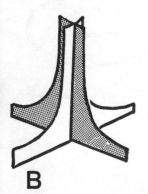

B

Procedure

- Fold four pieces of paper in half. Make the first pattern cutting a curved edge away from the fold. (Figure A)
- Cut four the same size.
- Glue these together to make a stand. (Figure B)
- Make a loop of a pipe cleaner at the top and insert in folds; staple for a secure hold.
- Slide pipe-cleaner-filled straws through the loop.
- Twist pipe cleaner ends to hold straws at four ends.
- Practice drawing four-season symbols on scrap paper

first. Draw on colored construction paper and cut out. Secure with thread to the ends of the straws. Move straws back and forth until balance is obtained.

- The completed kinetic can be sprayed one color or three different colors can be used: one for the base, another for the symbols, and still another for the straws. (Figure C)

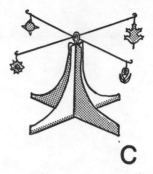

C

Lesson 10 Kinetic—Pariscraft Bird

Objectives

Discovering a balance point and at the same time thinking in terms of such a design is the focus of this lesson. Plan the project by first making a sketch and then creating it in three-dimensional form.

Materials

Pariscraft, water, newspapers, waxed paper, scissors, paints (acrylic or spray), marker.

Procedure

- Decide the length and depth of the bird by drawing it in profile first.
- Place newspaper on table and cover with waxed paper.
- Cut strips of pariscraft and smooth over the waxed paper in a little larger size than the bird pattern. Use three layers and cut two patterns.
- While pariscraft is damp, lift off waxed paper and join the top edges with strips of pariscraft. Immediately curve over so it looks like an inverted canoe. Let dry.
- Either make a cone of newspaper or use a milk-shake container and cover it with pariscraft.
- When both the bird and cone are dry. leave white and with paint or marker draw in the eye, bill, and feathers.

- Place the body of the bird on the cone shape and balance it. A little rocking motion will make the bird move back and forth for a short while. This is the basic principle of kinetics. (Figure A)

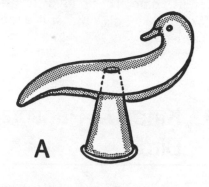

A

Bonus Ideas

Mobile—Scrap Collage with Textures

Collect contrasting textures, considering their weight in the balancing procedures of mobile making. Think of pleasing color, shape, and texture qualities.

Mobile—Wire and Foil

Curl wire into spiral shapes, tie a strip of foil in the center, and crush into balls. Make large and small ones. Balance the balls with different colored wire.

Mobile—Christmas Cards

Sort out a variety of Christmas cards and place on the table for balance. Consider having small cards at the top increasing in size or vice versa. Consider color as well—all green and red or an all gold or silver theme.

Mobile—Paper Cups and Paper Baking Cups

The many varieties of paper cups offer a challenge to mobile making. Inverting a paper cup and gluing a flattened paper baking cup on top immediately makes an interesting unit to work with. Glue two cups together, rim to rim, for another unit. Create your own and experiment with a totally balanced mobile.

Stabiles—Wallpaper Abstracts

Old wallpaper books are available free upon request at wallpaper stores. These contain a wealth of material with which to make stabiles. Decide on your theme and pattern. Glue two sides together and while damp form into shapes. Let dry and assemble.

Stabile—Sawdust and Wallpaper Paste Shapes

Make the paste mixture so it is easy to model. The cookie cutter with its many shapes is good for less motivated children; however, it is best to try for originality first. Place waxed paper on table to press the mixture on, cut into forms or model in the hand. While material is damp, push string into the center, let dry, and create your stabile.

Stabile—Stitchery Butterflies on Screening

Any subject can be used; however, butterflies are easy to draw and their colorful designs are appealing. Use branches in selected graceful forms, embed in a block of plasticine, add birds that were stitched on screening and then cut out.

Kinetic—Branches, Paper, and Tissue Shapes

Cut a variety of construction shapes: ovals, squares, circles, etc., making two of each. Place brightly colored tissue paper in between and paste together, securing threads to each. Form and arrange the branches in a stabile, then add the moving forms just created.

Kinetic—Macaroni, Coat Hanger, and Paper

Shape the coat hanger and embed hook in a clay base. Glue threads to macaroni and arrange in pleasing balance.

Kinetic—Cardboard and Seed Mosaic

For the stationary frame use cardboard design. Cut cardboard shapes and add a mosaic design on each side with colored seeds; these are lightweight and will move easily. Add threads and complete unit.

Index